W9-BBS-607

Advances in Developing Human Resources

Number 6, 2000

Richard A. Swanson
Editor-in-Chief

Developing High-Performance
Leadership Competency

Elwood F. Holton III & Sharon S. Naquin, Editors

AHRD
THE ACADEMY OF HUMAN RESOURCE DEVELOPMENT

BK

BERRETT–KOEHLER COMMUNICATIONS, INC.

Advances in Developing Human Resources (ISSN 1523-4223) is a quarterly monograph series published by the Academy of Human Resource Development and Berrett-Koehler Communications, Inc.

Academy of Human Resource Development
P.O. Box 25113
Baton Rouge, LA 70894-5113

Berrett-Koehler Communications, Inc.
450 Sansome Street, Suite 1200
San Francisco, CA 94111-4825

Subscription Orders: Please send subscription orders to Berrett-Koehler Communications, PO Box 565, Williston, VT 05495, or call 800-929-2929, or fax 802-864-7626. Subscriptions cost $79 for individuals and $125 for institutions. All orders must be prepaid in U.S. dollars or charged to Visa, MasterCard, or American Express. For orders outside the United States, please add $15 for surface mail or $30 for air mail. Librarians are encouraged to write for a free sample issue.

Editorial Correspondence: Address editorial correspondence and inquiries to Richard A. Swanson, Editor-in-Chief, *Advances in Developing Human Resources*, University of Minnesota, 1954 Buford Avenue, Suite 425, St. Paul, MN 55108, USA. E-mail: raswanson@uswest.net

 Printed in the United States of America on acid-free and recycled paper.

Postmaster: Please send address changes to the Berrett-Koehler address above.
Cover Design: Carolyn Deacy Design, San Francisco, CA
Production: Pleasant Run Publishing Services, Williamsburg, VA

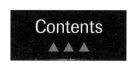
Contents

Preface   v

This issue and the competency framework it explores are the result of a rather unique field research project. A team of faculty and human resource development (HRD) Ph.D. students from Louisiana State University worked with an organization in Baton Rouge, Louisiana, for several years. The project had two parts. The first part was to develop a strategic plan for the HRD department that would transform it from a traditional training organization into a performance-based department. One key element of the plan that emerged was the development of an institute that would develop managers into leaders who could lead people to achieve high performance. The managers were seen as pivotal in transforming the organization, so they were given high priority. The second part of the project was to return with a new team of faculty and Ph.D. students to develop a competency framework to guide the development of high-performance leaders. This issue is a product of the second part of the project.

Building this model broke new theoretical ground. We could not find any evidence that anyone previously had attempted to define leadership behaviors using performance theory. We were committed not only to breaking new theoretical ground but also to making the theory accessible to practitioners in the form of a competency model. The challenge of creating new theory and making it useful for practice was both exhilarating and exhausting, and ultimately extremely rewarding.

This issue presents the competency model. Chapter One discusses the performance-leadership disconnect and the methodology used to create the model. Chapters Two through Four describe the full competency model, focusing on the organization, process, and individual levels of performance, respectively. Each chapter fully describes the competencies required at each level, along with supporting research and literature. Tables in each chapter present the competency groups, the 63 competencies, and the 180 subcompetencies. Chapter Five discusses the process for converting the general competency model into a leadership development program in a specific organization.

The High-Performance Leadership Development Team
(in alphabetical order):

Carson R. Arnett	Janis S. Lowe
Debora E. Baker	Susan A. Lynham
Mary A. Boudreaux	Lori Marjerison
Doris B. Collins	Sharon S. Naquin
Mertis Edwards	Marie B. Walsh
Elwood F. Holton III	Lynda S. Wilson

Chapter 1

▲ Performance-Driven Leadership Development

Elwood F. Holton III
Susan A. Lynham

High-Performance Leadership. Leading and managing people and organizational systems to achieve and sustain high levels of effectiveness by optimizing goals, design, and management at the individual, process, and organization levels.

It is generally accepted that leadership can make a difference (Bass, 1990; Burke & Day, 1986; Clark, Clark, & Campbell, 1992). However, the research, which is deep and diverse, is generally inconclusive as to which specific leadership skills are most effective. A leading scholar has commented:

> The field of leadership is presently in a state of ferment and confusion. Most of the theories are beset with conceptual weaknesses and lack strong empirical support. Several thousand empirical studies have been conducted on leadership effectiveness, but most of the results are contradictory and inconclusive....The confused state of the field can be attributed in large part to the disparity of approaches, the narrow focus of most researchers, and the absence of broad theories that integrate findings from the different approaches [Yukl, 1989, p. 253].

The purpose of this issue is to address these shortcomings. It presents a detailed competency framework that merges leadership research with performance improvement theory. This work differs from other work on leadership and leadership development in the following ways:

Integrates multiple leadership perspectives. Most work has focused on one specific aspect of leadership. This framework integrates disparate

1

streams of leadership research into a broad and holistic model for developing high-performance leadership competencies.

Uses a performance lens. Although many different lenses have been used to examine leadership, no previous work has systematically built a leadership development model through an organizational performance lens.

Grounded in theory and research. The methodology used to build this competency model began with research and theory. The best research and theory was selected and then assessed for practicality, assuming that the model is grounded in both theory and practice.

Translates research into specific competencies. This work translates research and theory on leadership into a practical framework and competency model suitable for curriculum design.

The remainder of this chapter discusses the disconnect between performance theory and leadership development, briefly reviews the leadership development literature, describes the development process for the competency model presented in Chapters Two through Four, and describes the structure for the issue.

Applying Performance Theory to Leadership Development

Leadership and leadership development have been defined in multiple ways. We use the following definitions:

Leadership: "A process whereby individuals influence groups of individuals to achieve shared goals or commonly desired outcomes" (Northouse, 1997).

Leadership development: "Every form of growth or stage of development in the life-cycle that promotes, encourages, and assists the expansion of knowledge and expertise required to optimize one's leadership potential [and performance]" (Brungardt, 1996, p. 83).

Reviews of leadership research (Bass, 1990; Fleishman et al., 1991; Yukl, 1989; Yukl & van Fleet, 1992) point out that leadership has been studied from many perspectives. A comprehensive literature review found sixty-five taxonomies of leader behavior published in the prior fifty years (Fleishman et al., 1991). The major approaches to leadership study have been identified as the power-influence approach, managerial behavior approach, trait approach, situational approach (nine different ones including path-goal, situational leadership, contingency theory, and leader-member exchange), and transformational or charismatic leadership (for example, the Burns theory of transforming leadership and Bass's theory of transformational leadership) (Yukl, 1989).

One controversy in the leadership literature concerns the distinction between leadership and managerial behaviors. Since 1977, conventional wisdom has been that leaders and managers are different types of people, with managers most concerned with how things get done and leaders with building commitment and vision (Kotter, 1990). A more recent way of characterizing the distinction between management and leadership is to contrast transformational and transactional leadership (Bass, 1985). As Yukl (1989) said, "Nobody has proposed that managing and leading are equivalent, but the degree of overlap is a point of sharp disagreement (p. 253)."

We prefer the most recent approach, described as the full range of leadership model (Avolio, 1999; Bass, 1998). Essentially this model acknowledges that leader and manager behaviors are different, but all leaders display both types of behavior to varying degrees, and transformational leadership augments transactional leadership. In our view, leadership for high performance integrates elements of what have traditionally been called leadership and managerial behaviors. As individuals rise to higher levels of formal leadership in organizations, the balance between leader and manager behavior certainly shifts, but we see few instances where a person can develop leadership skills without also being competent at managerial functions. In simple terms, the skills are different but complementary.

Performance theorists generally take a holistic systems view of organizational performance, although each discipline has defined performance in ways that suited its unique perspectives (Holton, 1999). Researchers have attempted to simplify organizational system complexity by developing taxonomies of key factors that influence performance. Two prominent performance models are the Rummler and Brache (1995) model and the Swanson (1996) model. The Rummler and Brache (1995) model of performance improvement was selected as the framework to guide this work because it is a more general model of organizational performance and offers a somewhat simpler fit to the leadership literature. In addition, some initial work linking the model to other foundational research had already been done (Wimbiscus, 1995).

Rummler and Brache provide an integrated framework for achieving competitive advantage by learning how to manage organizations, processes, and individuals effectively. Beginning with a holistic view of the organization, they set forth a rational, clear, and simple view of the organizational skeleton, process levels, and interdependencies. Their model hypothesizes that organizational failure is due not to lack of desire or effort, but lack of understanding of the variables that influence performance, which they call "performance levers" (1995, p. 2). A complete understanding and holistic management of these variables should result in high performance.

To guide the management of organizations as systems, Rummler and Brache provide the nine-cell matrix shown in Table 1.1. Three levels of performance are identified (organization, process, and individual) and three performance variables (goals, design, and management). For each cell they also identified key questions, which are shown in the table.

If these cells represent key performance levers, then it would seem logical that high- performance leadership might be defined by integrating them with leadership theory. Thus, the model provides a lens through which leadership variables affecting organizational performance were assessed.

It is particularly striking that no leadership model could be located that was grounded directly in systems theory, which has become the standard approach for improving organizational effectiveness and is deeply embedded in human resource development and organization development best practices (Cummings & Worley, 1997; Swanson, 1999). Simplistic performance models have led to the proliferation of "quick fixes" and faddish improvement programs, most of which focus on only a single element or a subset of performance variables. To develop leaders capable of leading complex organizational systems, leadership development should be embedded in a system's framework.

By using a performance model as the macrolens, leadership research was more systematically embedded in systems theory. The twenty-eight questions within the nine-cell matrix were used as the conceptual frame to transform the leadership research into applicable leadership competencies. We used a behavioral approach because we were most interested in defining competencies that leaders should develop to lead organizations to high performance. With the competencies, the nine-cell performance matrix could then be used to form an integrated curriculum, grounded in leadership and performance theory.

▲ Table 1.1 Rummler and Brache Performance Matrix

	Goals	Design	Management
Organization	• Has the organization's strategy/direction been articulated and communicated? • Does the strategy make sense, in terms of the external threats and opportunities and the internal strengths and weaknesses? • Given this strategy, have the required outputs of the organization and the level of performance expected from each output been determined and communicated?	• Are all the relevant functions in place? • Are all functions necessary? • Is the current flow of inputs and outputs between functions appropriate? • Does the formal organization structure support the strategy and enhance the efficiency of the system?	• Have appropriate function goals been set? • Is relevant performance measured? • Are resources appropriately allocated? • Are the interfaces between function steps being managed?

(Continued)

▲ Table 1.1 Continued

	Goals	Design	Management
Process	• Are goals for key processes linked to customer and organization requirements?	• Is this the most efficient/effective process for accomplishing process goals?	• Have appropriate process subgoals been set? • Is process performance managed? • Are sufficient resources allocated to each process? • Are the interfaces between process steps being managed?
Individual	• Are job outputs and standards linked to process requirements (which are in turn linked to customer and organization requirements)?	• Are process requirements reflected in the appropriate jobs? • Are job steps in a logical sequence? • Have supportive policies and procedures been developed? • Is the job environment ergonomically sound?	• Do the performers understand the Job Goals (outputs they are expected to produce and the standards they are expected to meet)? • Do the performers have sufficient resources, clear signals and priorities, and a logical job design?

- Are the performers rewarded for achieving the Job Goals?
- Do the performers know if they are meeting the Job Goals?
- Do the performers have the necessary skills and knowledge to achieve the Job Goals?
- If the performers were in an environment in which the five questions listed above were answered "yes," would they have the physical, mental, and emotional capacity to achieve the Job Goals?

Source: Rummler and Brache (1995). From *Improving performance: How to manage the white space on the organizational chart.* Copyright © 1995. Reprinted by permission of Jossey-Bass, Inc., a subsidiary of John Wiley & Sons, Inc.

Leadership Development

Although the general leadership literature is deep, the literature on leadership development is not. There is a deficiency of scholarly knowledge about leadership development in spite of an increasing drive for and investment in leadership development in organizations (Boyett & Boyett, 1998; Clark & Clark, 1994; McCauley, Moxley, & Van Velsor, 1998). As Fiedler (1996) stated, "We know very little about the processes of leadership and managerial training that contribute to organizational performance" (p. 244). Interestingly, a similar lament was offered many years ago when one author stated that "the hard fact remains that the effect of much of management development has been impressively negligible" (Bennett, 1959, p. 9).

In fact, there is relatively little emphasis in the literature on developmental processes for leaders. For example, one of the leading books summarizing leadership research devotes only one out of thirty-seven chapters in a twelve-hundred-page book to developmental processes (Bass, 1990). Also, the Center for Creative Leadership, which has been at the forefront of work on leadership development, only recently published a summary of its methods (McCauley et al., 1998). Yet it has been suggested recently that one core competency of effective leaders is the ability to develop other leaders at all levels of an organization (Tichy, 1997).

The body of knowledge pertaining to leadership development seems to reside in three key areas (Bass, 1990; Boyett & Boyett, 1998; Brungardt, 1996; Gardner, 1990; Jackson, 1993; Northouse, 1997; Schreisheim & Nieder, 1989; Yukl & van Fleet, 1992). The first area focuses on general approaches to leadership. A second area is that of leadership development research, most of which falls into four categories: early childhood and adolescent development, the role of formal education, adult and on-the-job experiences, and specialized leadership education (Bass, 1990; Brungardt, 1996; Clark & Clark, 1994; Hughes, Ginnet, & Curphy, 1993). The third area is that of leadership education research, which covers leadership development in elementary and secondary education contexts, higher education, training programs, and among senior citizens (Bass, 1990; Brungardt, 1996).

Two noteworthy works on leadership development are Brungardt (1996), who appears to be the first to try to gather this body of knowledge, and McCauley et al.'s (1998) *Handbook of Leadership Development.* A synthesis of the literature identified eight core knowns about leadership development (Lynham, 2000):

1. It occurs in early childhood and adolescent development.
2. Formal education plays a key role.
3. On-the-job experiences are important.
4. It occurs through specialized leadership education.
5. Leadership education focuses on three specific areas: improving a leader's attitudes, skills, and knowledge; training in success and effectiveness as a leader; and training and education on leadership styles (Bass, 1990).
6. There are a number of factors that can act as potential barriers to its effectiveness.
7. It is a lifelong process.
8. It is often confused with management development.

The Leadership Development-Performance Problem

Surprisingly, there is no clarity or agreement on the intended outcome of leadership development, raising a serious question about what the outcomes of this field are intended to be. Is its dependent variable one of individual growth and development or one of performance? The literature highlights outcomes of leadership development as including improved subordinate and human relationships; improved attitudes, skills, and knowledge; improved trainee leadership and group effectiveness; how to use major styles; improved decision-making style; sensitizing trainees to their management role; and developing and sharing personal and organizational vision (from key studies highlighted in Bass, 1990; Clark & Clark, 1994; McCauley et al., 1998).

The link joining leadership, leadership development, and performance seems to lie more in belief than in justifiable evidence (Meindl & Ehrlich, 1987; Bass, 1990). Nowhere is there a definition of leadership, and by association leadership development, that includes "for improving performance" as a core dependent variable. Rather, performance improvement is inferred, implied, and assumed as an outcome of leadership and leadership development. Given the increasing investment in leadership development by American organizations as well as organizations worldwide, this is a particularly troublesome void. Without a real, justified link between leadership development and performance, the field will likely continue to reflect an empirically inadequate framework for thought and practice.

Furthermore, most of the research conducted in leadership development is linked to specific models of leadership (for example, trait theory, behavior theory, or situational theory), yet leadership development encompasses many of these models and theories. This specificity of leadership models and theories raises the question of whether research findings on the effectiveness of specific leadership theories will hold true when developed in combination with multiple and sometimes contradictory leadership theories. For example, can it be assumed that because some studies show a positive correlation between transformational leadership theories and group performance that the same positive correlation can be assumed when this theory or model is merely a component of a larger, more comprehensive leadership development process?

This lack of theoretical integration is one reason there has been a trend toward developing integrated leadership frameworks (Canella & Monroe, 1997; Fleishman et al., 1991; Hooijberg, Hunt, & Dodge, 1997; Yukl, 1989). Thus, there appears to be some recognition that piecemeal approaches to studying and defining leadership are insufficient. Integrated models of leadership embrace the full range of what are often called management behaviors as well as the more visionary and transformational components of leadership (Schriesheim & Neider, 1989).

Building a Performance-Based Leadership Competency Framework

The fact that performance improvement theory has not been used as an organizing framework for leadership seems to be a glaring oversight, particularly given the concerns about leadership development theory. If there is confusion about the effectiveness of leadership and leadership development, then one logical direction of inquiry would be to connect leadership and performance theory. Recent work suggests that more organizational focus is needed in leadership research and that most of the research had not placed leadership in the larger organizational milieu in which it exists (House & Aditya, 1997). It seems logical that performance improvement theory might provide a rich perspective that had been overlooked in the literature and would also provide an integrated framework that could include management and leadership behaviors.

It was these observations that started us on the path of developing the High-performance Leadership Model. Lynham (1997) began a similar journey when she proposed a conceptual framework of how the Swanson (1996) performance model might be integrated into a model of responsible leadership for performance. She argued that leadership needs to focus on adding value to the organizational system by optimizing performance at the organizational, work process, group, and individual levels. However, she noted that leadership for performance has the potential to become abusive, so she also argued that responsible leadership for performance should balance three core elements: effectiveness, ethics, and endurance (White-Newman, 1993).

Because our goal was to create a framework that could be used to develop leaders, we decided to create a competency model that would integrate performance and leadership theory and facilitate developing high-performance leadership. Competency models have become a popular approach to leadership and management development. Competencies are less specific than tasks but more job related than learning objectives alone. Furthermore, they are ideally suited for multirater assessment (such as 360-degree feedback).

The competency framework presented here was developed through a rigorous research process. Imperative to the project's success was linking two streams of literature: (1) performance improvement and (2) leadership and management. Following are some key elements of the development process.

Research-Based Competency Development

Traditional competency development methods would have led the team to use current managers as subject matter experts to identify needed competencies. Although that approach has its place, we wanted to build a curriculum that could transform leadership development practice. Thus, the team made a key decision in the beginning to use research and theory to develop the competencies rather than starting with practice. This was a deliberate decision to develop a model of the way the research says leadership should be, rather than one that reflected current practice.

Grounding in Macro Performance Theory

We decided to use the Rummler and Brache (1995) performance model as the macro frame for competency development. Three research teams were formed and assigned a performance level (organization, process, or individual). Throughout the project, they became experts in the literature supporting each level.

Cell-Level Analysis

Each team extensively researched each cell (goals, design, management) within its level using key reviews as starting points (Fleishman et al., 1991; Ruona & Lyford-Nojima, 1997; Wimbiscus, 1995; Yukl, 1989). The key questions that Rummler and Brache identified within each cell were used to guide investigations into the research. Thus, the Rummler and Brache performance model was broken into its component parts, and leadership competencies were created that addressed the core questions for each cell.

Content Validation

Two key steps were taken to increase the content validity. First, each group's work was shared with other teams weekly, and with feedback obtained. The other groups served as both a sounding board and validity check. All group members were either practicing leaders in senior-level positions or had held significant managerial roles. Thus, they helped validate other groups' work from both a research and practice perspective. In some cases, groups redirected their work based on these reviews.

Second, the competency statements were audited using multiple lenses of an organization developed by Morgan (1997) to check for blind spots in the model. This step was taken because performance theory can sometimes seem too mechanistic and behavioristic. Morgan describes organizations using eight different lenses that he called metaphors (organizations as machines, organisms, brains, cultures, political systems, psychic prisons, flux and domination, and domination). His framework was selected because it appeared to be useful for checking the comprehensiveness of the competencies. Each competency was audited to determine the lens or lenses to which it closely corresponded. The result was a conceptual map that allowed the team to consider the relative weighting of the competencies within each organizational lens.

Linking the Cells and Levels

Once each cell and each level had been researched, the focus shifted to creating clear links between the performance levels to ensure they became more integrated. This step completed the inquiry development cycle that began by breaking the performance model into its component parts, researching them thoroughly, and then linking them back together for an integrated whole.

Overview of the Model

The integrated whole that emerged is portrayed in Figure 1.1. The nine-cell performance model used as the theoretical frame was transformed into a different structure to organize the leadership competencies better. It is important to remember that although the structure appears different, each cell of the Rummler-Brache model is addressed by this competency model. The model is organized into five layers (the first three layers are shown in Figure 1.1):

1. *Performance levels:* Three levels representing the three performance levels (organization, process, individual)
2. *Competency domains:* Six domains, two per performance level
3. *Competency groups:* Twenty-three competency groups, with three to five groups per domain
4. *Competencies:* Sixty-three competencies within the twenty-three competency groups
5. *Subcompetencies:* 180 subcompetencies spread across the 63 competencies

Subsequent chapters describe the competency domains, competency groups, competencies, and subcompetencies for the organization, process, and individual levels.

▲ Figure 1.1 Overview of the Competency Model

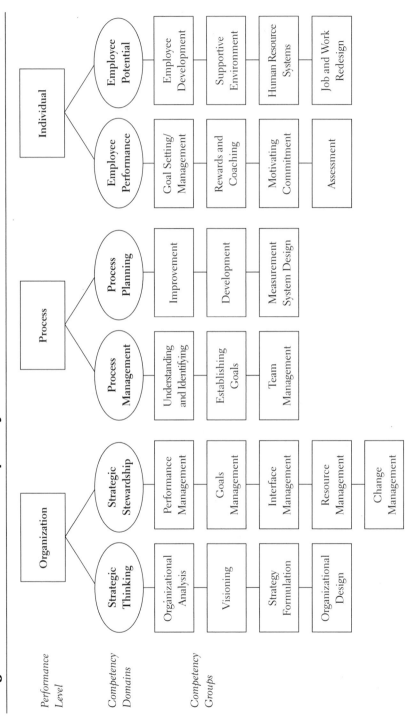

References

Avolio, B. J. (1999). *Full leadership development: Building vital forces in organizations.* Thousand Oaks, CA: Sage.

Bass, B. M. (1985). *Leadership and performance beyond expectations.* New York: Free Press.

Bass, B. M. (1990). *Bass and Stodgill's handbook of leadership: Theory, research, and managerial application.* New York: Free Press.

Bass, B. M. (1998). *Transformational leadership: Industrial, military, and educational impact.* Mahwah, NJ: Erlbaum.

Bennett, W. E. (1959). *Manager selection, education, and training.* New York: McGraw-Hill.

Boyett, J., & Boyett, J. (1998). *The guru guide: The best ideas of the top management thinkers.* New York: Wiley.

Brungardt, C. (1996). The making of leaders: A review of the research in leadership development and education. *Journal of Leadership Studies, 3*(3), 81–95.

Burke, M. J., & Day, R. R. (1986). A cumulative study of the effectiveness of managerial training. *Journal of Applied Psychology, 71,* 242–245.

Canella, A. A., Jr., & Monroe, M. J. (1997). Contrasting perspective on strategic leaders: Towards a more realistic view of top managers. *Journal of Management, 23,* 213–237.

Clark, K. E., & Clark, M. B. (1996). *Choosing to lead* (2nd ed.). Greensboro, NC: Center for Creative Leadership.

Clark, K. E., Clark, M. B., & Campbell, D. P. (Eds.). (1992). *Impact of leadership.* Greensboro, NC: Center for Creative Leadership.

Cummings, T., & Worley, C. (1997). *Organization development and change.* Cincinnati, OH: South-Western College Publishing.

Fielder, F. E. (1996). Research on leadership selection and training: One view of the future. *Administrative Science Quarterly, 41,* 241–250.

Fleishman, E. A., Mumford, M. D., Zaccaro, S. J., Levin, K. Y., Korotkin, A. L., & Hein, M. B. (1991). Taxonomic efforts in the description of leader behavior: A synthesis and functional interpretation. *Leadership Quarterly, 2,* 245–287.

Gardner, J. W. (1990). *On leadership.* New York: Free Press.

Holton, E. F. III (1999). An integrated model of performance domains: Bounding the theory and practice. *Performance Improvement Quarterly, 12* (3), 95–118.

Hooijberg, R., Hunt, J. G., & Dodge, G. E. (1997). Leadership complexity and development of the leaderplex model. *Journal of Management, 23*, 375–408.

House, R. J., & Aditya, R. N. (1997). The social scientific study of leadership: Quo vadis? *Journal of Management, 23*, 409–473.

Hughes, R. L., Ginnett, R. C., & Curphy, G. J. (1993). *Leadership: Enhancing the lessons of experience.* Homewood, IL: Irwin.

Jackson, C. N. (1993). On linking leadership theories. *Journal of Management Education, 17* (1), 67–78.

Kotter, J. P. (1990). *A force for change: How leadership differs from management.* New York: Free Press.

Lynham, S. A. (1997). The development and evaluation of a model of responsible leadership for performance: Beginning the journey. *Human Resource Development International, 1*, 207–220.

Lynham, S. A. (2000). Leadership development: A review of the theory and literature. In P. Kuchinke (Ed.), *Proceedings of the 2000 Academy of Human Resource Development Annual Meeting.* Baton Rouge, LA: Academy of Human Resource Development.

McCauley, C. D., Moxley, R. S., & Van Velsor, E. (Eds.). (1998). *The Center for Creative Leadership handbook of leadership development.* San Francisco: Jossey-Bass.

Meindl, J. R., & Ehrlich, S. B. (1987). The romance of leadership and the evaluation of organizational performance. *Academy of Management Journal, 30*(1), 91–109.

Morgan, G. (1997). *Images of organizations.* Thousand Oaks, CA: Sage.

Northouse, P. G. (1997). *Leadership: Theory and practice.* Thousand Oaks, CA: Sage.

Rummler, G. A., & Brache, A. P. (1995). *Improving performance: How to manage the white space on the organizational chart.* San Francisco: Jossey-Bass.

Ruona, W. E. A., & Lyford-Nojima, E. (1997). Performance diagnosis matrix: A discussion of performance improvement scholarship. *Performance Improvement Quarterly, 10*(4), 87–118.

Schriesheim, C. A., & Neider, L. L. (1989). Leadership theory and development: The coming of a new phase. *Leadership and Organization Journal, 10*(6), 17–26.

Swanson, R. A. (1996). *Analysis for improving performance: Tools for diagnosing organizations and documenting workplace expertise.* San Francisco: Berrett-Koehler.

Swanson, R. A. (1999). Foundation of performance improvement and implications for practice. In R. J. Torraco (Ed.), *Advances in developing human resources, 1* (pp. 1–25). San Francisco: Berrett- Koehler.

Tichy, N. M. (1997). *The leadership engine: How winning companies build leaders at every level.* New York: HarperBusiness.

White-Newman, J. B. (1993). *The three F's of leadership: A model and metaphor for effective, ethical and enduring leadership.* Unpublished manuscript. St. Paul, MN: College of St. Catherine.

Wimbiscus, J. J., Jr. (1995). A classification and description of human resource development scholars. *Human Resource Development Quarterly, 6,* 5–34.

Yukl, G. (1989). Managerial leadership: A review of theory and research. *Journal of Management, 15,* 251–289.

Yukl, G., & van Fleet, D. D. (1992). Theory and research on leadership in organizations. In M. D. Dunnette & L. M. Hough (Eds.), *Handbook of industrial and organizational psychology* (Vol. 3, pp. 147–197). Palo Alto, CA: Consulting Psychologists Press.

Chapter 2

▲ High-Performance Leadership at the Organization Level

Doris B. Collins
Janis S. Lowe
Carson R. Arnett

The Problem and the Solution. High-performance leaders must have competencies to lead organization-level goal setting, design, and management. This chapter describes two competency domains, strategic thinking and strategic stewardship, and nine competency groups that leaders must master to achieve high performance in an organization. These competencies address Rummler and Brache's (1995) organization level of performance.

According to Rummler and Brache (1995), "If executives [leaders] do not manage at the organization level, the best they can expect is modest performance improvement. At worst, efforts at other levels will be counterproductive" (p. 33). Using the key questions shown in Chapter One, an integrated framework for the development of high-performance leaders capable of meeting current and future organizational level challenges was developed (see Figure 2.1). The competencies are grouped into two domains: strategic thinking and strategic stewardship.

There are three fundamental assumptions of this high-performance leadership competency model. First, the future will be characterized by rapid, discontinuous change (Nadler et al., 1995). Second, the model assumes that the ultimate goal of an organization is fulfillment of its mission and satisfaction of its stakeholders. Third, leadership development processes improve the skills or change the behavior of individual leaders. By blending strategic thinking and strategic stewardship, high-performance leaders meet the challenges of managing discontinuous change, fulfilling the organization's mission, satisfying stakeholders, improving

▲ **Figure 2.1   Overview of the Organization-Level
Competency Domains and Groups**

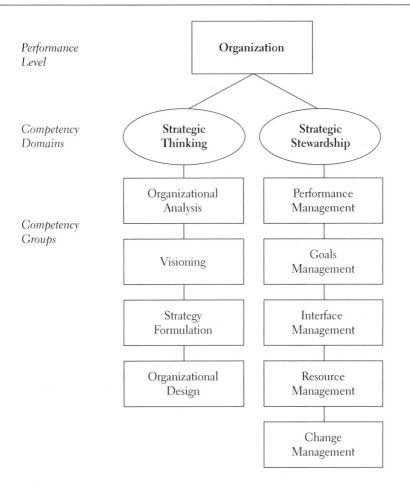

productivity, and improving the ability to achieve valued organizational outcomes.

Strategic Thinking

Strategic thinking incorporates strategic thought and action (Bryson, 1995), beginning with the older concept of strategic planning but extending it through a system's view of strategic management. High-performance leaders maintain the capacity to innovate, an element crucial to organizational success (Eadie, 1997), by integrating strategic thinking into the organization. In the high-performance competency model, strategic thinking comprises four competency groups: organizational analysis, visioning, strategy formulation, and organizational design.

Organizational Analysis

To understand the organization's purpose and assess environmental forces, high-performance leaders engage the organization in organizational analysis, a systematic information-gathering process. The organizational analysis is the foundational step that enables the organization to identify its strategic issues, which leads to the development of a compelling and effective strategy. High-performance leaders must initiate a strategic planning process and assess the organization's external and internal environment to complete an organizational analysis (see Table 2.1).

Initiating a Strategic Planning Process (1.1)

Developing a new organizational strategy requires that high-performance leaders obtain agreement from stakeholders to undertake a strategic planning process and develop a plan for planning. To *build acceptance of the strategic planning process as a method to improve the organization,* leaders address the purpose of the effort, the process steps, reporting methods of strategic action, individual and group roles, and the commitment of resources (Bryson, 1995). Senior leaders champion the strategic planning process because they are the change agents who set the tone for what happens in the rest of the organization at the organization, process, and individual levels. Therefore, high-performance leaders *clarify the organizational mission and values, including basic beliefs, values, priorities, and public image,* with the strategic planning team.

Assessing External and Internal Environment (1.2)

After the stakeholders agree to a strategic planning process as a method to improve the organization, the high-performance leader explores the external and internal environment in order to *distinguish strengths, weaknesses, opportunities, and threats.* During the external assessment,

▲ Table 2.1 Organizational Analysis Competencies

Number	Competency		Subcompetency
1	Organizational Analysis		
1.1	Initiates and champions a strategic planning process	1.1a	Builds acceptance of the strategic planning process as a method to improve the organization
		1.1b	Clarifies organizational mission and values, including basic beliefs, values, priorities, and public image
1.2	Assesses the organization's external and internal environment	1.2a	Distinguishes the strengths, weaknesses, opportunities, and threats of the organization as they relate to individuals, processes, and stakeholders
		1.2b	Synthesizes feedback on the impact of political, economic, social, and technological forces and trends; key resource controllers; and competitors, collaborators, and customers (external environment)
		1.2c	Synthesizes feedback on the impact of people, economic information, work processes, information technology, competencies, culture, performance, and organizational strategy (internal environment)

these leaders *synthesize feedback on the impact of political, economic, social, and technological forces and trends; key resource controllers; and competitors, collaborators, and customers.* Assessment of the internal environment involves a *synthesis of the impact of people, economic information, work processes, information technology, competencies, culture, performance, and organizational strategy.* The high-performance leader analyzes the sources of each external and internal force to identify strategic issues and develops a new strategy to attain desired outcomes consistent with the organization's mission and goals (Porter, 1980; Wright, Pringle, & Kroll, 1992). After the organization analysis is complete, the organization is ready to begin developing a vision.

Visioning

A vision paints a picture of what the organization should look like after it successfully implements its strategies. A clear vision guides and coordinates the decisions and actions of everyone working in the organization. Table 2.2 outlines competencies required for high-performance leaders to create a shared vision and develop a compelling future state for the organization.

Creating Shared Vision (2.1)

A clear vision provides the context for everything else that happens within the organization (Albrecht, 1994). The high-performance leader *knows alternative approaches to determining a vision* other than the typical structured strategic planning process (such as future search or Delphi technique). Because the same technique will not work every time, it is critical that the leader adapt the appropriate visioning method to the needs of the organization.

A shared vision incorporates results of the organizational analysis and translates those results into action. To develop a shared vision, the high-performance leader identifies stakeholders and *collaborates with those stakeholders to design a vision that is more desirable than the current organizational vision.* Once stakeholders are identified, leaders use a variety of communication and collaboration methods to build rapport and establish relationships with them. By involving stakeholders in describing the future state of the organization, leaders *build support for the acceptance*

▲ **Table 2.2 Visioning Competencies**

Number	Competency		Subcompetency
2	Visioning		
2.1	Creates a shared vision of the organization that incorporates the results of the external and internal assessment	2.1a	Knows alternative approaches to determining a vision
		2.1b	Collaborates with stakeholders to design a vision for the organization that is more desirable than the current vision
		2.1c	Builds support for acceptance of the new organization vision
2.2	Specifies future state of the organization's core processes	2.2a	Differentiates how all parts of the organization interact, operate, and affect one another
		2.2b	Describes organizational grouping alternatives and linking mechanisms to achieve valued outcomes

of a new organizational vision. Actual deep-seated commitment to the vision statement emerges over time.

Specifying a Future State of the Organization's Core Processes (2.2)

High-performance leaders develop a picture of what the future organization's core processes should look like and how it should function to achieve the outcomes expected from the organization's core processes. To describe a new vision for the future, high-performance leaders *differentiate how all parts of the organization interact, operate, and affect one another* (Nanus, 1996); understand how outcomes affect core processes; and know the structure of all business units. These leaders also recognize the need for structural change and *describe organizational grouping alternatives and linking mechanisms to achieve valued outcomes.*

Strategy Formulation

Through collaborative efforts, strategy formulation identifies the strategic issues (fundamental policy questions or critical challenges) that affect the organization, creates action plans, and determines the appropriate culture to achieve the organization mission. Table 2.3 lists the competencies for high-performance leaders to develop effective strategies that enable the organization to remain competitive in a continuously changing environment.

Identifying Strategic Issues (3.1)

The identification of strategic issues is the heart of the development of a new strategic direction. High-performance leaders *integrate information from the external and internal environmental analysis into the strategy formulation process to identify the strategic issues that affect the operation of the organization.* They also *gather information through gap analysis to contrast the current state of the organization and the future vision for the organization.* The gap analysis and the results of the environmental assessment alert the organization to the strategic issues that must be resolved in order to remain competitive in a changing environment. Identification of strategic issues enables high-performance leaders to frame issues so employees understand that an alternative course of action (strategy) is needed.

▲ **Table 2.3 Strategy Formulation Competencies**

Number	Competency		Subcompetency
3	Strategy Formulation		
3.1	Identifies strategic issues for the organization	3.1a	Integrates information from the external and internal analysis to identify strategic issues
		3.1b	Gathers information from an analysis of the gap between the current state and the future vision for the organization
3.2	Determines courses of action for resolving strategic issues	3.2a	Formulates alternatives incorporating environmental analysis, gap analysis, and organizational design considerations
		3.2b	Identifies potential barriers to implementing the new strategy and determines methods for overcoming those barriers
3.3	Creates and maintains a culture of effective and ethical performance	3.3a	Uses leadership role to define an organizational culture that supports high performance
		3.3b	Ensures that a new strategy is implemented and performance goals are achieved with the highest standards of ethics and integrity

Determining Courses of Action to Resolve Strategic Issues (3.2)

High-performance leaders collaborate with stakeholders to resolve strategic issues by *formulating alternatives that incorporate environmental analysis, gap analysis, and organizational design considerations.* They go one step further and evaluate how each alternative may affect critical organizational systems. In assessing alternative courses of action, high-performance leaders evaluate such elements as human resources, financial resources, core processes, and strategic partnerships. In addition, they include performance indicators in the strategic plan along with goals, objectives, and courses of action so that effective measurement is built into strategy.

High-performance leaders also collaborate with stakeholders to *identify potential barriers to implementing new strategy and determine methods to overcome those barriers.* Although it is not necessary to eliminate barriers fully early in the strategic planning process, identifying them early helps to minimize implementation difficulties.

Creating a Culture of Effective and Ethical Performance (3.3)

In high-performance organizations there is a strong relationship among culture, leadership, and performance (Hesselbein, Goldsmith, & Beckhard, 1996). High-performance leaders shape the social fabric of the organization by *using leadership roles to define an organizational culture that supports high performance.* They make sense of organizational complexity and provide direction and energy to colleagues and subordinates. They become visible role models and send clear signals concerning the kind of organization they want, the key values they promote, and the behaviors expected (Nadler & Tushman, 1988). High-performance leaders constantly advocate and evaluate core values. As a result, employees make better decisions because they focus on those clear values and beliefs that identify with the organization's core values.

High-performance leaders also *ensure that a new strategy is implemented and performance goals are achieved with the highest standards of ethics and integrity.* That is, they are fair and respectful of others, professionally responsible for their actions, respectful of the worth and dignity of all people, and seek to contribute to the welfare of not only those in the organization but also to the larger community and society (Bergmann, Hurson, & Russ-Eft, 1999; Lynham, 1997). High-performance leaders believe in honest, ethical business dealings, keeping promises, and admitting mistakes. They communicate their priorities, values, and concerns openly and honestly, establish measures that encourage ethical action throughout the organization, and reward ethical behavior formally and informally. The conduct of the leader assures customers that the organization has ethical business practices and is worthy of trust (Nadler et al., 1995).

Organizational Design

When determining courses of action to resolve strategic issues, high-performance leaders also consider an appropriate organizational design. Intricately linked with both strategic thinking and strategic stewardship, organizational design is diagnostically driven and results in changes to the formal organization structure. According to Nadler and Tushman (1988), such changes ensure that new strategy is implemented throughout the system and has the greatest potential to improve performance. Leaders concerned with organizational performance understand that the different components of an organization must be properly organized for optimal performance (Rummler & Brache, 1995).

Strategic leaders diagnose problems, formulate a design intent, devise a concrete list of design criteria, and construct, assess, and refine a full range of grouping and linking alternatives (Nadler & Tushman, 1997). In considering strategic and operational needs, high-performance leaders develop the design from the top down to implement strategy and from the bottom up to develop work processes and create meaningful and motivating jobs for individuals. They know that modifications in structure and process directly alter patterns of activity and behavior, leading to improved performance (Nadler & Tushman, 1997). Table 2.4 provides an overview of the competencies necessary for high-performance leaders to design the best organizational structure.

Designing the Appropriate Structure (4.1)

Strategy drives the organizational design process, balanced by informal organizational elements and individual concerns. In formulating new strategies, high-performance leaders envision the new structure before actually designing the organization. They search for a good fit among the elements of strategy, task, individual, and formal and informal organizational arrangements when making decisions about formal structures and

▲ Table 2.4 Organizational Design Competencies

Number	Competency		Subcompetency
4	Organizational Design		
4.1	Considers strategic and operational needs to design an appropriate organizational structure	4.1a	Distinguishes criteria for directing and assessing the design effort based on results of the organizational analysis
		4.1b	Identifies broad information processing needs for each grouping and linking alternative
4.2	Evaluates design implications while considering alternative designs	4.2a	Assesses design alternatives for fit with organizational components
		4.2b	Determines the links in the informal organizational structure that are appropriate to the new strategic design

processes (Nadler & Tushman, 1997). These elements form the *distinguishing criteria for directing and assessing the design effort based on results of the organizational analysis.*

High-performance work is organized around processes and multi-skilled work groups that require significant interaction to achieve effective results. When considering the basic structure of the organization, high-performance leaders must *identify the broad information processing needs for each grouping and linking alternatives* aimed at providing that interaction. They must also consider strategic and operational needs, as well as the alignment of organizational components when creating new organizational design alternatives. Since achieving and sustaining high performance often means substantial change to work design, they must consider innovative strategic designs such as network organizations, joint ventures, strategic alliances, and flat structures (Nadler et al., 1992) as ways to structure and link groups throughout the organization.

Evaluating Design Alternatives (4.2)

High-performance leaders *assess each design alternative for fit with organizational components* and *determine the links in the informal organizational structure that are appropriate to the new strategic design.* They also assess the alignment of organizational strategy, work systems, management processes, and organizational culture and climate to ensure optimal response to customer requirements and environmental demands (Semler, 1999). When considering design alternatives, Nadler and Tushman (1997) caution that although the line between design and implementation is fuzzy, the thought process prior to implementation is the most important factor in the development of a design. Consequently, high-performance leaders create two implementation plans: a transition plan that focuses on the technical and social issues of the organization and an execution plan that maps specific steps for implementing the transition plan and putting the new organizational structure in place.

Strategic Stewardship

The concept of strategic stewardship combines Webster's (1987) definition of stewardship—"the activities of a person in charge of an estate or the activities of a person administering finances or property" (p. 587)—with Vaill's (1998) idea of managerial leadership where leadership and management cannot be separated. Strategic stewardship is the capacity to implement plans developed during strategic thinking processes to produce the high levels of effectiveness that define superior organizations (Eadie, 1997). The remainder of Chapter Two discusses the five competency groups within strategic stewardship: performance management, goals management, interface management, resource management, and change management.

Performance Management

Swanson defines performance as "the valued output of a system in the form of goods or services" (1999, p. 5). Rummler and Brache (1995) describe measurement (assessment) as the foundation for performance management and the single greatest determiner of an organization's effectiveness as a system. Performance management measures the valued output against the strategic goals of the organization and, depending on the results, formulates action plans to correct or improve performance. High-performance leaders believe in continuous improvement, which is a result of continuous assessment of the organization's performance (Bates, 1999). Assessment results provide leaders the impetus to take action such as communicating revised goals, redefining roles, and reallocating resources. Table 2.5 provides an overview of the competencies necessary for high-performance leaders to manage organizational performance.

Leading Assessment of Organization's Strategies (5.1)

High-performance leaders ensure that the organization's system for measuring activities, services, or products reflects its strategy. Two of the most powerful progress and outcome measurement systems are the performance matrix (Rummler & Brache, 1995) and the balanced scorecard (Kaplan & Norton, 1996). By advocating assessment as a linked series of activities across time, these systems make both substandard performance and goal accomplishment easily identifiable.

Using the measurement dimensions established in the organizational strategy, high-performance leaders establish data collection mechanisms for tracking actual performance (Rummler & Brache, 1995). They use

▲ **Table 2.5 Performance Management Competencies**

Number	Competency		Subcompetency
5	Performance Management		
5.1	Leads groups or individuals in periodic assessments of the organization's strategies and their relation to core processes and organization design	5.1a	Determines whether processes and the process owners have met performance indicators
		5.1b	Institutionalizes a performance measurement system that links critical dimensions of performance within and between all levels of the organization
5.2	Initiates corrective action when performance is not tracking with goals	5.2a	Diagnoses and applies the appropriate intervention to the negative performance level and situation
		5.2b	Revises strategic thinking methods based on periodic assessment
5.3	Optimizes organization's overall performance	5.3a	Identifies key linkages and critical dimensions of performance for achieving organizational outcomes
		5.3b	Delegates decision-making authority to the point of service impact

performance data to *determine whether the process and process owners have met expectations by monitoring performance indicators* and assessing results for strategic impact.

As assessment becomes a systematic and continuous organizational process for performance measurement, review, and improvement efforts, high-performance leaders *institutionalize a performance measurement system that links critical dimensions of performance within and between all levels of the organization.* They use communication, collaboration, reward systems, praise, and mentoring to champion the success of the measurement system and correct its deficiencies. The key is to use assessment information to reconfigure the organization's strategy, core processes, and work design as the environment, customer requirements, or work technology changes.

Initiating Corrective Action (5.2)

When performance assessment information is fed back to relevant individuals, units, or subsystems, high-performance leaders fulfill their coaching and development role by discussing corrective action if performance is off-target. The leader *diagnoses the cause of the negative performance and applies the appropriate intervention* to correct specific performance problems.

High-performance leaders recognize that assessment serves as a catalyst for organizational renewal. They continually *revise strategic thinking methods based on periodic assessment* and incorporate double-loop learning in the assessment processes. They determine the best strategy development process for the organization and adjust strategy processes when needed to cultivate a continuous quality improvement mind-set.

Optimizing Organization Performance (5.3)

High-performance leaders continuously review organizational systems searching for opportunities to increase performance. They *identify key linkages and the critical dimensions of performance for achieving organizational outcomes* (Kaplan & Norton, 1996), such as financial, internal business, customer perspective, employee learning and growth, and employee empowerment. Leaders incorporate the key linkages in goals and subgoals set in collaboration with process owners and individual employees.

To improve organizational performance in a customer-driven environment that requires faster, more reliable service at lower cost, high-performance leaders *delegate decision-making authority to the point of service impact.* They give workers the authority to make decisions within the boundaries of the organization mission and goals.

Goals Management

Goals management affects core process outputs and determines how boundaries in the organizational system affect organizational and process performance. Collaborative links across process owners, groups, and levels enable high-performance leaders to manage organizational goals. Table 2.6 provides an overview of the competencies necessary for high-performance leaders to manage goals.

Leading Development of Goals and Objectives (6.1)

For a competency-based organization to work, every level needs clear direction and well-defined decision rights outlined through subgoals (Limrick & Cunnington, 1993). High-performance leaders *align goals and objectives with specific strategies and results of core processes* to ensure that the organization will achieve its valued outcomes. In addition, their organizations *develop subgoals to support the achievement of the overall goals* (Rummler & Brache, 1995). As part of the strategy implementation process, high-performance organizations link the subgoals of all levels of the organization or risk decreasing the effectiveness and efficiency of the organization in accomplishing its purpose.

Leading Strategy Implementation Process (6.2)

Creating a strategy is not enough: "The changes indicated by adopting new strategies must be incorporated throughout the system for them to be brought to life and for real value to be created for the organization and its stakeholders" (Bryson, 1995, p. 36). High-performance leaders are more successful in implementing strategy when they *prioritize action plans, generate a detailed implementation schedule,* and provide a measurement system that is routinely monitored. These action plans contain *midterm goals that provide manageable steps and benchmarks for change*

▲ Table 2.6 Goals Management Competencies

Number	Competency		Subcompetency
6	Goals Management		
6.1	Leads development of goals and objectives that are aligned with external and internal realities	6.1a	Aligns goals and objectives with specific strategies and results of core process
		6.1b	Develops subgoals to support achievement of overall organization goals
6.2	Leads implementation of organizational strategy that directly affects outcomes at the organization, process, and individual levels	6.2a	Prioritizes action plans and generates detailed implementation schedule
		6.2b	Develops midterm goals that provide manageable steps and benchmarks for change
		6.2c	Coordinates roles and responsibilities of oversight bodies, process owners, process managers, organizational teams, and individuals, paying attention to the technical and social organizational issues

and provide the leader an opportunity to change directions if the new strategy is not working as anticipated.

High-performance leaders *coordinate the roles and responsibilities of the oversight bodies, process owners, process managers, organizational teams, and individuals, paying attention to both technical and social organizational issues* involved in implementing strategy. They understand the unique needs of processes and work groups and take these into account when giving clear directions on what needs to be done, by whom, and by what date. Successful strategy implementation depends primarily on the use of formal and informal mechanisms to promote implementation-centered discussions, decision making, problem solving and conflict management (Bryson, 1995). High-performance leaders address social issues during strategy implementation by managing interfaces or encouraging collaboration within the organization.

Interface Management

According to Rummler and Brache (1995), "The greatest opportunities for performance improvement lie in the functional interfaces–those points at which the baton [work] is being passed from one department, process team, or individual to another" (p. 9). Ashkenas, Ulrich, Jick, and Kerr (1995) call these "boundaries," defining four types of boundaries that must be successfully dealt with in achieving high-performance organizations:

- Vertical boundaries between levels and ranks of people
- Horizontal boundaries between functions and disciplines
- External boundaries between the organization and its suppliers, customers, and regulators
- Geographic boundaries between nations, cultures, and markets.

All levels of management and leadership affect how organizational boundaries operate, and those boundaries affect the work of everyone in an organization. Therefore, high-performance organizations focus their efforts on how to permeate those boundaries: to move ideas, information, decisions, talent, and actions to where they are most needed. High-performance leaders manage these functional interfaces or boundaries by communicating strategy and performance information to relevant subsystems, supporting collaboration that leads to valued outcomes for external and internal customers, and promoting the organization to external entities. (See Table 2.7 for an overview of competencies.)

▲ Table 2.7 Interface Management Competencies

Number	Competency		Subcompetency
7	Interface Management		
7.1	Communicates strategy and performance information to relevant subsystems throughout the organization	7.1a	Selects appropriate communication channels, modes, venues, and styles
		7.1b	Shares information, new ideas, and practices that span the vertical and horizontal boundaries between processes
		7.1c	Builds dialogue and encourages people to question organizational decisions
7.2	Supports collaboration to provide efficient and effective organizational performance that leads to valued outcomes for external and internal customers	7.2a	Encourages input, rewards employees for ideas on improving organizational performance, and creates realistic suggestion systems that include action and feedback loops
		7.2b	Communicates with and engages all process owners, stakeholders, and employees to commit to the mission and goals of the organization
7.3	Presents and promotes the organization to external entities	7.3a	Represents organizational interests to external groups with oversight responsibilities and other constituents
		7.3b	Works with customers to ensure the organization meets their needs

Communicating Strategy and Performance Information (7.1)

Effective communication skills enable high-performance leaders to manage the "white space" between functions and business units of the organization (Rummler & Brache, 1995). They *select the appropriate communication channels, modes, venues, and styles* that most effectively communicate strategy, issues, and performance information throughout the organization (Rummler & Brache, 1995). They also *share information, new ideas, and practices that span vertical and horizontal boundaries between processes* and clarify the relationships of each process owner to those boundaries.

Communication skills are important for leaders in minimizing organizational conflict. To communicate effectively throughout the organization, high-performance leaders *build dialogue and encourage people to question organizational decisions.* Communication about organizational decisions and the resolution of conflicting agendas are critical components of high-performance organizations that prevent the organization from sending mixed messages to the process and individual levels concerning vision and direction.

Supporting Collaboration (7.2)

Since leadership is accomplished through people, collaboration permeates high-performance organizations. It is, in effect, the lifeblood of the organization, carrying the information and innovation "nutrients" to and through every cell and carrying away the conflict inherent in any human organization. Collaboration and effective communication among levels, groups, process owners, individuals, and stakeholders and across vertical, horizontal, external, and geographic boundaries are among the most critical competencies in creating high-performance organizations. These organizations support collaborative efforts that enhance organizational performance by *encouraging input, rewarding employees for ideas on improving organizational performance, and creating realistic suggestion systems that include action and feedback loops.*

Horizontal boundaries present especially difficult challenges in communication and collaboration. High-performance leaders form process action teams with executive sponsors and *communicate with all process owners, stakeholders, and employees to obtain their commitment to the mission and goals of the organization.* By making sure that employees hear about the proposed changes many times across multiple channels, they inspire employees to identify with the leader's vision and reinforce the need for a new strategic direction.

Promoting the Organization to External Entities (7.3)

Governing structures differ, but most leaders report to an external body or governing board, or they may be required to organize and present the organization's collective thought and action to an interorganization network (Bryson, 1995). Regardless of the type of organization governance, to be successful high-performance leaders must have the skills to *represent organizational interests to external groups with oversight responsibilities and to other constituents.* Ultimately it is these leaders' responsibility to "sell" what is happening in the organization to all entities. Leaders are more successful when they build an image of what the organization can contribute that is meaningful and worthwhile and share the image internally and externally.

Another key to organizational success is the satisfaction of its customers. High-performance leaders *work with customers to ensure that the organization meets their needs.* If an organization does not know what criteria customers use to judge the organization and how the organization is performing against those criteria, there is little likelihood that it will know what it should do to satisfy its customers (Boschken, 1994).

Resource Management

Leaders use resource allocation to support strategic objectives. They know how to allocate people, equipment, information, and budget across the system in order to meet organization and core process goals and objectives. They also know how to acquire resources and identify resource constraints. Resource management includes both the coordination of resources and the creation of an environment where staff develop skills to accomplish the organization's core process goals and objectives. Because of the rapidly changing nature of industry and escalating global competitive pressures, high-performance leaders are being forced to attend more aggressively and self-consciously to the learning skills of their staff and organization. These leaders view individual, group, and organizational learning as a fundamental mechanism by which their organization reacts with its environment, processes information, and adapts to changing external and internal conditions (Dirkx, 1999) (see Table 2.8 for competencies).

▲ Table 2.8 Resource Management Competencies

Number	Competency		Subcompetency
8	Resource Management		
8.1	Coordinates resources for accomplishment of organizational strategy	8.1a	Identifies resources needed to implement strategy
		8.1b	Acquires physical, human, financial, and information resources and allocates them across the entire system to accomplish organization and core process goals and objectives
		8.1c	Distributes technical competence and leadership skills throughout all levels of the organization
8.2	Creates an environment for staff to develop appropriate skills to accomplish organizational and core process goals and objectives	8.2a	Encourages employees to set personal goals that improve organizational performance and to develop new competencies and skills
		8.2b	Champions continuous learning as organizational learning style and experiments with different methods for individual, group, and organizational learning

Coordinating Resources (8.1)

Adequate resource allocation enables each function to achieve its goals, thereby making its expected contribution to the overall performance of the organization. High-performance leaders begin resource allocation by *identifying resources needed to implement strategy* and determining sources from which to obtain them. They know how to *acquire physical, human, financial; and information resources and allocate those resources across the entire system to accomplish organization and core process goals and objectives* (Rummler & Brache, 1995). They also allocate resources by *distributing technical competence and leadership skills throughout all levels of the organization.*

Creating Environment for Staff to Develop Skills (8.2)

Learning organizations require continuous development of support systems for organizational, group, and individual learning (Kuchinke, 1995). High-performance leaders motivate individuals to grow, expose them to learning opportunities, and provide needed support. They encourage employees to inquire about and analyze decisions, *set personal goals that improve organizational performance, and develop new competencies and skills.* High-performance leaders *also champion continuous learning as the organizational learning style and experiment with different methods for individual, group, and organizational learning* to find the best method to accomplish the organization's core process goals and objectives. They build employee confidence by allowing employees to take risks and responsibility and back them up when they make mistakes (Heifetz & Laurie, 1997).

Change Management

Today's rapidly changing environment requires organizations to adapt, or they put their survival at risk (Conger, 1999). To respond effectively to the changing environment, high-performance organizations institutionalize change as a core value (Trahant & Burke, 1996) so that the organization is capable of rapid learning and adapting (Ackord, 1999). Yukl (1998) calls leading and managing change the essence of high-performance leadership. The art of leadership lies in balancing the demands of change against the need for people within the organization to feel valued and secure in order to produce their best work. High-performance leaders acquire the competencies outlined in Table 2.9 to balance those competing values effectively and lead change successfully.

Institutionalizing Change as a Core Value (9.1)

Some theorists believe that strategy promotes inflexibility, impedes the capacity of people in the organization to respond to changes in the environment, and breeds future resistance to change (Mintzberg, 1994; Mintzberg, Ahlstrand, & Lampel, 1998; The new breed, 1984; Steiner & Kunin, 1983). Yet global changes are forcing organizations to develop new strategies and learn new ways of operating. High-performance leaders challenge people's deeply held beliefs to *create a readiness for change*. They mobilize people throughout the organization to adapt to a continuously changing environment. Adaptive work is required when the values that made the organization successful become less relevant and when legitimate but competing perspectives emerge (Heifetz & Laurie, 1997). Mobilizing an organization to change basic values, beliefs, and attitudes is a critical challenge (Heifetz & Laurie, 1997) that requires a learning strategy that engages people in confronting challenges, adjusting their values, changing perspectives, and learning new habits (Eisenbach, Watson, & Pillai, 1999).

High-performance leaders *assist organizational members in overcoming resistance to change* by showing empathy and support, revealing results of the gap analysis, involving them in strategy formulation, and conveying a positive expectation for change (Cummings & Worley, 1997). They help people in the organization to collaborate, trust one another, and develop a collective sense of responsibility for the new direction and performance of the organization.

Building Coalitions (9.2)

High-performance leaders gain political support for organizational change efforts and *address the problems inherent in change of power, anxiety, and control*. Changing the organization often threatens the balance of power, resulting in political conflicts and struggles (Cummings & Worley, 1997). High-performance leaders become aware of the problems, build coalitions with individuals and business units throughout the

▲ Table 2.9   Change Management Competencies

Number	Competency	Subcompetency	
9	Change Management		
9.1	Institutionalizes change as a core organizational value	9.1a	Creates a readiness for change
		9.1b	Assists organization members in overcoming resistance to change
9.2	Builds coalitions with those who have a vested interest in the organization to support change efforts	9.2a	Addresses the problems inherent in any change of power, anxiety, and control
		9.2b	Influences people to commit to primary processes that affect outcomes, goals, and objectives
9.3	Plans and implements a transition to a future organizational state	9.3a	Determines specific activities and events that must occur if the transition is to be successful
		9.3b	Creates structure for managing the change process
9.4	Sustains change effort momentum by focusing on processes, individuals, and strategies	9.4a	Provides financial, technological, information, and human resources to sustain the change effort continually
		9.4b	Builds a support system for change agents
		9.4c	Reinforces new behaviors through rewards, recognition, encouragement, and praise
		9.4d	Provides training and encourages staff to use skills to meet the needs of the changing environment

organization, and include those individuals in championing and communicating the new strategy.

High-performance leaders *influence people to commit to primary processes that affect the organization.* They realize that not every stakeholder will agree on every set of strategies, but will more likely join a coalition in support of the planning and implementation of the new organizational vision if leaders listen to and value their ideas.

Planning and Implementing a Transition (9.3)

High-performance leaders involve those with a vested interest in planning and implementing a transition in strategy. Every high-performance organization needs leaders capable of managing the change process across the organization, process, and individual levels. As transition begins, high-performance leaders *determine the specific activities and events that must occur for the transition to be successful* and define a transition period during which the organization learns how to implement the plan to reach the desired future state (Cummings & Worley, 1997).

High-performance leaders obtain the support of people and groups prior to *creating the structure for managing the change process.* They are more effective in implementing strategy when change initiatives are linked to business units, functions, processes, and individuals and when they incorporate employees' interests in the strategy by creating opportunities to transfer skills across units. High-performance leaders continually revise, refine, and implement new strategies to meet the organization's needs in a fast-changing environment.

Sustaining Change Effort Momentum (9.4)

High-performance leaders sustain change effort momentum by increasing communication of the vision (Cummings & Worley, 1997), systematically planning and creating short-term wins, *providing additional financial, technological, information, and human resources specifically for the change effort,* and *building a support system for change agents.* Leaders continually encourage change agents and remind them of the positive reasons for establishing a new strategy. They also *reinforce new behaviors* in the organization and continually empower, support, and encourage employees to perform to the best of their ability, for themselves and for the organization.

To sustain the change effort momentum, high-performance organizations *provide necessary training and encourage staff to use skills fully to meet the needs of the changing environment.* Leaders provide the appropriate professional training and development for employees so that they can perform effectively and to their highest potential.

Summary

High-performance leaders have to be proficient in strategic thinking and strategic stewardship. The competencies required to be an accomplished leader in a high-performance organization are complex and overlapping. To be an effective strategist, high-performance leaders must have the competencies necessary to enable them to fulfill missions, meet their mandates, and satisfy constituents in a continuously changing environment. Both strategic thinking (formulating plans, setting goals, and establishing structures) and strategic stewardship (the capacity to implement plans and reach outcomes) are necessary to produce the high level of effectiveness that defines superior organizations. Collaboration permeates high-performance organizations at all levels and throughout all competency areas. By blending competencies for strategic thinking and strategic stewardship, high-performance leaders will achieve the mission of the organization.

References

Ackord, R. (1999). Transformational leadership. *Strategy and Leadership, 27*(1), 20–25.

Albrecht, K. (1994). *The northbound train: Finding the purpose, setting the direction, shaping the destiny of your organization.* New York: American Management Association.

Ashkenas, R., Ulrich, D., Jick, T., & Kerr, S. (1995). *The boundaryless organization.* San Francisco: Jossey-Bass.

Bates, R. (1999). Measuring performance improvement. *Advances in Developing Human Resources, 1,* 47–67.

Bergmann, H., Hurson, K., & Russ-Eft, D. (1999). *Everyone a leader: A grassroots model for the new workplace.* New York: Wiley.

Boschken, H. L. (1994). Organizational performance and multiple constituencies. *Public Administration Review, 54*, 308–312.

Bryson, J. (1995). *Strategic planning for public and nonprofit organizations: A guide to strengthening and sustaining organizational achievement.* San Francisco: Jossey-Bass.

Conger, J. (1999). *Leader's change handbook.* San Francisco: Jossey-Bass.

Cummings, T., & Worley, C. (1997). *Organization development and change.* Cincinnati: South-Western College Publishing.

Dirkx, J. (1999). Managers as facilitators of learning organizations. *Human Resource Development Quarterly, 10*(2), 127–134.

Eadie, D. C. (1997). *Changing by design.* San Francisco: Jossey-Bass.

Eisenbach, R., Watson, K., & Pillai, R. (1999). Transformational leadership in the context of organizational change. *Journal of Organizational Change Management, 12*(2), 80–88.

Heifetz, R. A., & Laurie, D. L. (1997, January–February). The work of leadership. *Harvard Business Review,* 124–134.

Hesselbein, F., Goldsmith, M., & Beckhard, R. (1996). *Leader of the future.* San Francisco: Jossey-Bass.

Kaplan, R., & Norton, D. (1996). *The balanced scorecard: Translating strategy into action.* Boston: Harvard Business School Press.

Kuchinke, K. P. (1995). Managing learning performance. *Human Resource Development Quarterly, 6*(3), 307–316.

Limrick, D., & Cunnington, B. (1993). *Managing the new organization.* San Francisco: Jossey-Bass.

Lynham, S. A. (1997). The development and evaluation of a model of responsible leadership for performance: Beginning the journey. *Human Resource Development International, 1,* 207–220.

Mintzberg, H. (1994). *The rise and fall of strategic planning.* New York: Free Press.

Mintzberg, H., Ahlstrand, B., & Lampel, J. (1998). *Strategy safari.* New York: Free Press.

Nadler, D. A., Gerstein, M. S., & Shaw, R. B. (1992). *Organizational architecture: Designs for changing organizations.* San Francisco: Jossey-Bass.

Nadler, D. A., Shaw, R. B., & Walton, A. E. (1995). *Discontinuous change: Leading organizational transformation.* San Francisco: Jossey-Bass.

Nadler, D. A., & Tushman, M. L. (1988). *Strategic organization design: Concepts, tools and processes.* Glenview, IL: Scott, Foresman.

Nadler, D. A., & Tushman, M. L. (1997). *Competing by design: The power of organizational architecture.* New York: Oxford University Press.

Nanus, B. (1996). *Leading the way to organizational renewal.* Portland, OR: Productivity Press.

The new breed of strategic planner. (1984, September 7). *Business Week,* 62–66, 68.

Porter, M. (1980). *Competitive strategy: Techniques for analyzing industries and competitors.* New York: Macmillan.

Rummler, G., & Brache, A. (1995). *Improving performance: How to manage the white space on the organizational chart.* San Francisco: Jossey-Bass.

Semler, S. (1999). Operationalizing alignment: Testing alignment theory. In P. Kuchinke (Ed.), *Proceedings of the Academy of Human Resource Development.* Baton Rouge, LA: Academy of Human Resource Development.

Steiner, G., & Kunin, H. (1983). Formal strategic planning in the United States today. *Long Range Planning, 16*(3), 12–17.

Swanson, R. (1999). Performance improvement theory and practice. In R. J. Torraco (Ed.), *Advances in developing human resources, 1,* pp. 1–25. San Francisco: Berrett-Koehler.

Trahant, B., & Burke, W. B. (1996). Traveling through transitions. *Training and Development, 50,* 37–41.

Vaill, P. (1998). *Spirited leading and learning.* San Francisco: Jossey-Bass.

Webster's New World Dictionary (2nd College ed.). (1987). New York: Simon & Schuster.

Wright, P., Pringle, C., & Kroll, M. (1992). *Strategic management text and cases.* Needham Heights, MA: Allyn and Bacon.

Yukl, G. (1998). *Leadership in organizations.* Englewood Cliffs, NJ: Prentice-Hall.

▲ High-Performance Leadership at the Process Level

Debora E. Baker
Marie B. Walsh
Lori Marjerison

The Problem and the Solution. High-performance leaders must have competencies to lead process-level goal setting, design, and management. This chapter describes two competency domains, process planning and process management, and six competency groups that leaders must master to achieve high performance in an organization. These competencies address Rummler and Brache's (1995) process level of performance.

According to Rummler and Brache (1995), an organization is only as good as its processes. Organizational processes describe the work of an organization and are responsible for producing goods and services (that is, outputs) for customers. The Rummler and Brache model describes the cells of the process level to include: process goals, process design, and process management. High-performance leaders not only recognize these cells and the importance of processes in general; they also have the competencies needed to develop, strengthen, and maintain them. The result is a more complete and capable organization.

Much of the literature on processes is practitioner based; not much scholarly research has occurred in this area. The most recent and popular consideration of the process level is associated with the "quality movement," including Total Quality Management (TQM), continuous process improvement, quality circles, and related efforts (Hackman & Wagman, 1995). Identifying, understanding, and improving processes are the cornerstones of these programs. Juran (1992, 1993), Davenport

(1993), Harrington (1991), and other quality gurus have contributed heavily to the quality literature. At the practitioner level, a plethora of how-to guides and consultants have helped the business and government sectors incorporate more process-level management into organizations. With these guides as a foundation, the next step is to integrate and coordinate leadership of the organization's process level with other levels.

Competencies required to lead at the process level in an organization fall into two domains and six competency groups (see Figure 3.1). The first competency domain is process management, which includes process understanding and identification, process goals establishment, and team management. The second domain is planning for processes and includes process improvement, development, and measurement systems. These competencies are closely linked to the organization and individual levels. Consequently, there is deliberate overlap between the process competencies and the competencies in other levels of performance.

▲ **Figure 3.1   Overview of the Process-Level Competency Domains and Groups**

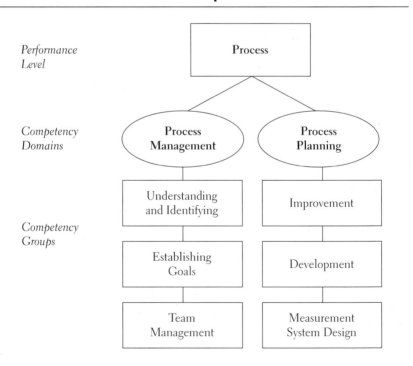

Process Management

An organization is composed of multiple processes of varying type and importance. The ability to distinguish between these processes, to develop and manage organizationally congruent goals, and to manage the human resources to support these processes are the fundamental competencies of the high-performance leader.

Understanding and Identifying Processes

Processes fall into categories based on role and function. Therefore, the first set of competencies for high-performance leadership calls for the leader to distinguish, identify, and consider different types of processes (see Table 3.1).

Understanding Types of Organizational Processes (10.1)

In the simplest terms, a work process is made up of steps, tasks, or activities having a beginning and end. This sequence of steps or activities converts inputs to an output by producing a tangible product or service. A work process adds value to the inputs by changing them or using them to produce something new (Galloway, 1994). Good managers or leaders should understand the processes critical to the success of their organization. However, many processes span organizational boundaries, diluting the responsibilities and knowledge of many managers or leaders. Moreover, there are different types of processes within any organization that may influence organizational functioning. The high-performance leader must be aware of the influences of these different types of processes and be able to differentiate between them.

High-performance leaders must be able to *differentiate primary, support, and management processes* (Rummler & Brache, 1995). Primary processes are those that result in a product or service that the organization's external customers receive. These primary processes should have a direct role in producing or fulfilling the organization's primary function. Support processes produce products that are invisible to external customers but are essential to the effective management of the business. The third category of processes, management processes, includes actions necessary to support the business functions. Identification of processes usually

▲ **Table 3.1 Process Understanding and Identification**

Number	Competency		Subcompetency
10	Process Understanding and Identification		
10.1	Understands types of organizational processes	10.1a	Differentiates primary, support, and management processes
		10.1b	Identifies macro- and microprocesses
10.2	Identifies organization's core and critical processes	10.2a	Identifies critical and core business processes for achieving strategic goals
		10.2b	Plans and implements management of critical processes

begins with typical business processes and how they fit into the process hierarchy (Harrington, 1991).

Leaders also need to be able to *identify macro- or microprocesses in the organization*. Macroprocesses generally involve many people and are cross-functional. These are the processes that cut across those silos of the organization. Smaller, more localized processes may be called micro-processes and often involve line workers (Galloway, 1994). The ability to distinguish between macro- and microprocesses becomes important for every level of process development and management.

Identifying Core Processes (10.2)

In addition to developing an inventory of business and management processes, the leader must *identify the organization's core and critical processes for achieving strategic goals* (Davenport, 1993; Harrington, 1991; Hunt, 1996). Typically three to seven processes are selected as being most critical to the implementation of the organizational goals and strategy (Rummler & Brache, 1995). In order to identify the core processes, the leader finds answers to questions such as, "What do we do as a business?" and "How do we do it?" (Harrington, 1991).

Critical processes are those that present serious dangers to human life, health, and the environment or that risk the loss of large sums of money (Juran, 1992). These *critical processes must be identified and adequate management processes planned and implemented*. Identification of core and critical processes for achieving strategic goals requires the leader to make the linkage from the strategic organizational level to the process level. The leader is called on to consider strategy and then identify or develop core processes that assist the organization in achieving those strategic goals.

Establishing Process Goals

The second group of competencies for high-performance leadership at the process level relates to establishing process goals. Once leaders have identified primary, support, management, core, and/or critical processes, they might be tempted to move their organizations directly toward establishing or improving those processes. However, to do so overlooks an important step. The Rummler and Brache model reminds us that goals should be established at every level and links among the levels established. The idea is that processes can benefit from the same attention to strategic focus that is more common at the organization level (see Table 3.2).

Obtaining Input for Development of Process Goals (11.1)

The five sources of input that have been identified to help organizations establish process goals translate to five subcompetencies. The first subcompetency is the ability to *obtain feedback from internal and external customers* (Davenport, 1993; Harrington, 1991; Juran, 1992). External customers are defined as those who purchase the product or service; internal customers use the product in their processes (Juran, 1992). This competency requires the leader to acquire knowledge related to effective methods for gaining feedback as well as the ability to identify internal and external customers. In turn, this should lead to more effective methods for gaining feedback, as well as the ability to analyze that feedback and convert it into strategy.

Second, leaders must *review their organization's strategy, design, and management to determine process goals.* This area of input moves the leader toward an important link between the other levels. Simply stated, process goals should support and mirror strategy. Equally important, they should consider the organization's design and management (Davenport, 1993). For the leader, this means analyzing the organization's strategy and its design. Then determinations may be made as to what implications that strategy and design might have for the way a process should work.

Third, critical business issues (CBIs) provide another area of input for process goals. Processes may need to be developed, revised, or strengthened based on current critical issues for the organization. This requires the leader to develop the ability to *prioritize and select core processes for improvement or redesign based on those that have the greatest impact on these critical business issues* (Davenport, 1995; Harrington, 1991). A dual understanding of CBIs and core processes is required, as well as an ability to relate how the potential improvements in core processes will advance strategy.

The fourth area of input for process goals relies on benchmarking information (Davenport, 1993; Juran, 1992). Juran reminds us that benchmarking an organization's processes against those of other organizations can provide important motivation for improving the effectiveness of processes. Benchmarking information may be based on the organization's performance objectives, or it may be based on "the best" in a specific process.

For leaders, this competency means *selecting and conducting the appropriate type of benchmarking for the process*. It may also mean developing a knowledge base regarding different types of benchmarking and selecting those that are most appropriate. The leader may need to learn various types of benchmarking, including internal, competitive, functional, and generic.

The ability to *gather historical performance information* provides the final area of input for process goals and calls for the leader to gather applicable historical information. Said differently, this area of input asks, "How well has this process performed in the past?"

Developing Process Goal Statements (11.2)

Once the input has been gathered, a second set of competencies for process goals comes into play: the development of goal statements. The leader should develop the ability to convert information from the five sources of input into goal statements. This requires the ability to *synthesize the information* (examine relationships, prioritize) followed by the ability to *establish measurable goal statements* (Davenport, 1993). Establishing measurable goal statements requires an understanding of goal measurement and frameworks for developing vision. Davenport (1993) provides a good outline for goal statements, calling for them to include vision, objectives, and attributes.

Managing the Impact of Process Goals (11.3)

Once goal statements have been developed, the next step is to *assess the impact of process goals on other organizational processes and functions*. This competency serves as a feedback loop to organizational-level strategic goals. The long-term benefit of the process depends on its effective relationship with the organizational processes and functions. Considering the impact of process goals may require the leader to look at technology and imposed mandates. Assessing the impact of process goals requires the leader not only to understand other processes and functions within the organization, but also to identify means by which they interface and affect each other.

▲ Table 3.2 Process Goals Establishment Competencies

Number	Competency		Subcompetency
11	Process Goals Establishment		
11.1	Obtains input for the development of process goals	11.1a	Implements effective methods for gaining feedback from internal and external customers
		11.1b	Reviews organization's strategy, design, and management to determine process goals
		11.1c	Prioritizes and selects core processes for process improvement or redesign based on which have the greatest impact on critical business issues
		11.1d	Selects and conducts the appropriate type of benchmarking
		11.1e	Gathers applicable historical performance information
11.2	Develops process goal statements	11.2a	Synthesizes customer and benchmarking feedback, strategic information, core process, operational assumptions, and historical process information
		11.2b	Establishes measurable process improvement goal statements for each process

11.3	Manages the impact of process goals	11.3a	Assesses the impact of process goals on other organizational processes and functions
		11.3b	Communicates goals to lower levels
		11.3c	Modifies process goals as organizational goals and requirements change

Just as process goals link to the strategic level by supporting strategic goals, they also link to the job and performer level through *communicating goals to lower levels.* For maximum performance, process goals are integrated into performance objectives at the group and individual levels. To do so requires competencies related to an understanding of the principles of delegation, organizational management, and design. It also requires the ability to communicate goals and vision in order to obtain buy-in.

The long-term benefit of process goals also relies on continual assessment of changing organizational goals and requirements. Such assessment should translate into modifications in process goals. Thus, a leader should develop the ability to *modify process goals as organizational goals and requirements change* (Davenport, 1993; Hammer, 1996). Rummler and Brache's key role for the leader, that of managing the interface between the cells, is important in the development of process goals because input and influence travel both horizontally and vertically in the organization (Juran, 1992).

Team Management

High-performance process leadership requires leading teams effectively. Teams can represent a wide variety of formats: loosely formed, project, self-managing, or parallel structures, for example. Strong processes require developing strong, effective teams and the ability to sustain and promote change. Thus, this competency group comprises four competencies: developing process teams, managing process teams, promoting responsibility for performance, and managing organizational change (see Table 3.3).

Developing Effective Process Teams (12.1)

High-performance leaders manage processes using steering committees, design teams, and process owners. The high-performance leader *selects process teams* by determining selection criteria for each role (Davenport, 1993; Harrington, 1991; Rummler & Brache, 1995). This requires the ability to differentiate the work of the committees, teams, and owners. At the same time, the leader must understand considerations regarding the design and implementation of processes. This will allow for the establishment of the best criteria to promote a strong match between design and team roles.

Once the roles have been identified, the leader's next step is to *identify, assign, or function as a process owner* (Hammer, 1996). Process owners play a key role because they assume responsibility for the process outcome. By ensuring accountability through process ownership, leaders eliminate many potential problems. "Someone must own the process and be accountable for it. If you review a process where responsibility has not been clearly assigned, or where roles and responsibilities have not been clearly defined and agreed to, you will find problems in that operation" (Lynch, 1996).

Although an individual process owner may maintain a certain level of accountability, processes thrive on teams. High-performance leaders *facilitate the process of team formation and maintenance* (Hammer, 1996) and develop skills related to managing those teams. Processes also thrive on teams with cross-functional representation. Although representatives from different areas make more diverse teams, leaders must understand and recognize potential problems associated with these teams.

Manages Process Teams (12.2)

The effective use of teams requires attention to preparing and developing staff to assume their roles as team members or as process owners. Therefore, high-performance leaders *initiate training for process owners and team members* (Harrington, 1991; Rummler & Brache, 1995). Equal attention must be given to *ensuring that the appropriate financial, personal, and other support mechanisms exist for carrying out process goals* (Hammer, 1993). The high-performance leader draws another important connection to the individual level by examining and developing staffing patterns to support the work of process teams.

Discussions of performance often focus on the mechanical aspects of production, but high-performance leaders understand that process performance takes place through people. Therefore, they continue to develop their staff through coaching, mentoring, and rewarding. They are able to assist process performers in resolving technical problems as well as team-related problems. To bring out the best performance in the team, the leader teaches the team to take care of the process *and* the group, identify and solve process problems, and resolve group conflicts.

The high-performance leader also wants cross-functional teams to eliminate destructive conflict. That means seeking common ground from among what may be diverse viewpoints and stakeholders. The team needs

▲ Table 3.3 Team Management Competencies

Number	Competency		Subcompetency
12	Team Management		
12.1	Develops effective process teams	12.1a	Selects process teams
		12.1b	Identifies, assigns, or functions as a process owner
		12.1c	Facilitates process team formation and maintenance to enhance process performance
12.2	Manages process teams	12.2a	Initiates training for process owners and team members
		12.2b	Obtains financial, personnel, and other support for goals
		12.2c	Resolves conflicts that arise in cross-functional team settings and seeks consensus among diverse viewpoints to build commitment
		12.2d	Interfaces and communicates with members of all parts of the process, particularly those separated by organizational boundaries

12.3	Promotes responsibility for performance	12.3a	Institutes mechanisms in the workplace to encourage process ownership and accountability
		12.3b	Uses the human performance system as a tool to ensure changes are supported by the work environment
12.4	Manages organizational change	12.4a	Assesses and confronts the organization's readiness for process change
		12.4b	Manages the human aspects of change in process improvement activities

a certain level of consensus among stakeholders so that each one is willing to invest in the process. Therefore, high-performance leaders maintain skills in *resolving conflicts that arise in cross-functional team settings and seeking consensus among diverse viewpoints in order to build commitment among stakeholders.* These competencies require extensive and effective communication. That means keeping teams and individuals updated and in the loop. High-performance leaders are able to *facilitate and communicate with all members of all parts of the process, particularly those separated by organizational boundaries* (Rummler & Brache, 1995).

Promoting Responsibility for Performance (12.3)

Effective processes are the product of an organization in which both individuals and teams accept responsibility. High-performance leaders *institute mechanisms in the workplace to encourage process ownership and accountability.* That translates into encouraging others to take ownership for work products and services, as well as holding appropriate individuals accountable. It also means selecting mechanisms that encourage process ownership and accountability.

As processes are implemented, the high-performance leader *uses the human performance system as a tool to ensure that changes are supported by the work environment* (Harrington, 1987, 1991). This is a critical link to the individual level. The performance level of the process is impeded when the team is not developed or designed in a manner that supports the process. The team's performance is impeded as well when it is not appropriately designed to support the process. The high-performance leader keeps these two systems synchronized so performance is maximized for both the process and the team.

Managing Organizational Change (12.4)

In today's information-driven work environment, the ability to manage change in an organization gains new importance. This skill is especially important in an organization that emphasizes processes. Referring back to competencies related to the development of process goals, one can see that process goals are based on information that changes or evolves. For example, feedback may indicate the need to modify products to meet the needs of internal and external customers better. Therefore, optimal performance means keeping processes flexible enough to respond to change. It may also mean developing new processes to support change. All of this leads to the need for a set of leadership competencies in the area of organizational change as it relates to processes.

Responding effectively to change means *assessing and confronting the organization's readiness for process change* (Rummler & Brache, 1995). To begin process change in an organization unprepared for change may limit the organization's effectiveness and waste resources. Leaders should understand concepts such as drivers of change and identify areas of resistance to change within the organization. Finally, they should be able to assess the political and cultural climate inside and outside the organization.

Finally, leaders must *manage the human aspects of change in process improvement activities* (Davenport, 1993; Rummler & Brache, 1995). Processes are developed, managed, and improved by teams of people. The leader who fails to appreciate the impact that change can have on those individuals and their performance ignores a significant barrier to process effectiveness. Leaders who want to maximize the performance of employees and processes move quickly to assess the impact of changes resulting from process improvement. Some leaders choose to mandate changes through a new policy or process. A more effective route might be to solicit the commitment of individuals and teams within the organization. To obtain buy-in, the leader needs to convey a need for change.

Process Planning

The high-performance leader incorporates the competencies of the process planning domain into the ongoing effort of the organization's processes. The competencies to actually develop processes, design and implement measurement and feedback systems, and recognize and seize improvement opportunities are critical to the high-performance leader.

Process Improvement

Not only is the concept of process improvement a pivotal part of the quality movement; it is also a competency required of the high-performance leader. The leader who wants maximum performance maintains competencies for process improvement. This translates into the four competencies shown in Table 3.4.

▲ Table 3.4 Process Improvement Competencies

Number	Competency		Subcompetency
13	Process Improvement		
13.1	Analyzes processes	13.1a	Identifies performance problems linked to processes
		13.1b	Selects subprocesses for performance and process improvement efforts
		13.1c	Selects process facilitators and consultants to guide and challenge senior management and process teams in improvement efforts
13.2	Prepares organization for process improvement or reengineering	13.2a	Evaluates appropriate process improvement or reengineering methodologies as related to processes selected for improvement activities
		13.2b	Creates the team infrastructure for process improvement or reengineering
		13.2c	Identifies enablers and constraints for process change

13.3	Designs or redesigns processes for improvement	13.3a	Assesses feasibility of process design alternatives and selects preferred design
		13.3b	Designs and develops a prototype of well-defined, unambiguous, and understandable process
		13.3c	Develops process subgoals for measurement
13.4	Effectively implements process changes	13.4a	Maintains the ability to develop migration strategies for new processes
		13.4b	Creates organizational systems for process improvement to maintain alignment between process and organizational goals

Analyzing Processes (13.1)

Analyzing processes can begin with an exercise such as *identifying performance problems linked to processes* (Davenport, 1995; Harrington, 1995). This competency requires the ability to distinguish between characteristics of effective and ineffective processes. High-performance leaders study the process, examining its effectiveness, characteristics, and results. After careful analysis, they *select subprocesses for performance and process improvement efforts.*

Leaders can assist their organizations in analyzing processes as an internal exercise. However, organizations may also find value in obtaining an outside consultant to analyze the organization's processes. Thus, in addition to maintaining their own skills related to analysis, leaders maintain skills in *selecting process facilitators and consultants to guide and challenge senior management's and process teams in improvement efforts* (Harrington, 1991).

Preparing for Process Improvement or Reengineering (13.2)

Once problems in processes have been identified, decisions should be made as to whether to seek process improvement or process reengineering. If the decision is to seek process improvement or reengineering, organizations will find a variety of methodologies for doing so. High-performance leaders understand those methodologies and maintain the ability to *evaluate them and make an appropriate selection.*

Another set of competencies involves preparing the organization to implement the chosen methodology. High-performance leaders remember that implementing process improvement or reengineering is a process in itself. Therefore, they *create the team infrastructure for the process improvement or reengineering* methodology selected. They also remember that process improvement efforts bring change, so they prepare their organization for process improvement by managing the change. They also analyze their organization, locating the *enablers of change for the methodology selected and any constraints to the methodology.*

Designing or Redesigning Processes (13.3)

Processes that prove ineffective, unresponsive, or problematic may require redesign or a new process. High-performance leaders are prepared for both and understand the steps for each. They also maintain an awareness or knowledge base of design alternatives and use that knowledge to *assess the feasibility of process design alternatives and select the preferred design* for the current situation (Davenport, 1993; Carr & Litman, 1990; Harrington, 1991).

First, knowledge must be acquired regarding assessment principles and methods. That knowledge is then converted to feasibility criteria, which are themselves converted to feasibility analysis. Often leaders test the process through the use of manual or computer-based process mapping, simulating new processes, and analyzing the organizational environment for new process workability.

Once problems have been identified, options explored, and design alternatives selected, the organization is ready to implement process design or redesign. The effective utilization of the newly designed or redesigned process depends on a well-articulated design. Therefore, high-performance leaders facilitate the *design and development of prototypes for well-defined, unambiguous, and understandable processes* (Davenport, 1993). To do so, they must understand the concept of and elements for a process prototype.

Finally, high-performance leaders want to ensure that methods exist for measuring the process's effectiveness after implementation. Therefore, they *develop process subgoals for measurement.* This competency requires the leader to understand the concept of subgoals and identify key process junctures and interim points where measurement may be applied.

Effectively Implementing Process Change (13.4)

Now that the process has been redesigned or a new process developed, assessed, and tested, consideration must turn to its effective implementation. The high-performance leader provides as much attention to this phase of process improvement as to the process design.

Effective implementation of processes first requires a plan. High-performance leaders *maintain the ability to develop migration strategies for new processes* (Davenport, 1995). They are knowledgeable regarding various migration strategies and appropriately link those strategies to new processes.

Equally important, high-performance leaders *create organizational systems for process improvement to maintain the alignment between process and organizational goals.* In other words, they maintain an organizational culture, structure, and system that is flexible enough to process improvements. To do so they keep process change improvements linked to organizational strategy. Moreover, they continually recognize opportunities for process and performance improvement.

Process Development

Once new process designs are complete, certain tools assist implementation. Leadership that appropriately identifies and uses process tools, institutes effective mechanisms for management, and facilitates comprehensive communication among groups maximizes the potential of new processes (see Table 3.5).

Effectively Using Process Tools (14.1)

The development of processes begins with the ability to *apply the appropriate process tools to design and/or improve processes* (Harrington, 1991). For the high-performance leader, this means becoming familiar with process maintenance and process design. Another category of tools are those related to process mapping. Process mapping tools permit process designers to *document and scope the "as is" and "to be" of process design* (Harrington, 1987; Hunt, 1996; Rummler & Brache, 1995). Process designers begin by establishing the framework for the process: its scope, functionality, and organizational impact. Mapping tools (both computer based and manual) may then be applied to begin design.

Designing and improving processes is facilitated by the ability to *deploy new technologies as required and available to improve and/or streamline processes.* This competency requires the high-performance leader to stay abreast of events, trends, and new tools. It also means maintaining an understanding of the current state of technology that may be useful in process improvement.

Effectively Managing Processes and Projects (14.2)

Establishing and designing new processes requires management and oversight just as the process itself will. Therefore, high-performance leaders *use project management tools and methodology to guide process*

▲ Table 3.5   Process Development Competencies

Number	Competency		Subcompetency
14	Process Development		
14.1	Uses process tools effectively	14.1a	Applies the appropriate process tools to design and/or improve processes
		14.1b	Documents and scopes "as is" and "to be" processes using process mapping tools
		14.1c	Deploys new technologies as required to improve and/or streamline processes
14.2	Manages process improvement projects effectively	14.2a	Uses project management tools and methodology to guide process improvement
		14.2b	Anticipates and plans for barriers to process improvement
14.3	Facilitates process-related communications	14.3a	Selects communication materials and mechanisms appropriate to the various stakeholders during process improvement activities
		14.3b	Obtains steering committee buy-in before new process implementation
		14.3c	Obtains top management support and solicits visible participation and buy-in

improvement efforts. These leaders acquire knowledge of different types of project management tools and maintain the ability to apply them.

Like other projects, unexpected barriers can derail the establishment of processes. Performance leaders *anticipate and plan for barriers to process improvement.* They maintain an awareness of organizational and industrial barriers and objections to change, integrate those barriers into their plans, and develop means for overcoming them.

Facilitating Process-Related Communications (14.3)

Beyond the technical competencies needed for designing processes, communication competencies are needed to ensure the effective implementation of the process. High-performance leaders know how to ensure that the appropriate stakeholders remain informed and involved during design, approval, and implementation. To do so, they *select communication materials and mechanisms appropriate to the various stakeholders during process improvement activities* (Juran, 1992). Thus, leaders need to know best practices for communicating process change.

Once the process design is complete, approval from various groups may be required. High-performance leaders strategically identify those groups, including the steering committee and top management. They *obtain steering committee buy-in before new process implementation* and *obtain top management support and solicit visible participation and buy-in* (Hammer, 1996). Both of these competencies require knowledge of stakeholder issues and skills in politics, negotiation, and interpersonal influence.

Measurement System Design

Effective processes depend on comprehensive and continual systems of measurement and feedback. Leaders who implement these systems strengthen processes and maximize their continued high performance. High-performance leadership requires a wide variety of competencies that range from understanding measurement concepts, to establishing measurements, to making them understandable and accessible (see Table 3.6).

Instituting Measurement Systems (15.1)

High-performance leaders should first *understand the concept of process measurement*, including statistical controls and quality control measures,

▲ Table 3.6   Measurement System Design Competencies

Number	Competency		Subcompetency
15	Measurement System Design		
15.1	Institutes measurement system	15.1a	Understands and establishes a process measurement that includes statistical controls and quality control measures
		15.1b	Integrates customer needs and other stakeholder requirements into the measurement system
		15.1c	Converts goals to subgoals and incorporates them into the measurement system
		15.1d	Breaks down overall process measurement architecture such that teams and individuals can use them
15.2	Institutes feedback systems	15.2a	Monitors process performance and initiates process improvement efforts as needed to ensure continued process performance and improvement
		15.2b	Designs feedback systems

and then establish quantitative measurements. The leader must establish a measurement system that *integrates customer needs and stakeholder requirements* and links with process goals. Then the high-performance leader *establishes quantitative measurements for process goals* (Harrington, 1991; Rummler & Brache, 1995). By understanding concepts of measurement and using statistical controls as appropriate, the leader then takes those goals and *converts them to process subgoals, incorporating them into the measurement system.* An earlier competency highlighted the need to keep stakeholders involved in other aspects of process design and development. The same holds true for effective measurement.

The next step is to ensure that the measurement system is understandable and usable on the application level. To do so, leaders *break down overall process measurement architecture such that teams and individuals can use them.* The idea is to develop better-understood performance measures more directly associated with the actual work. For the high-performance leader, this competency is supported by a knowledge of performance measurement architecture, the ability to define measurements in an understandable manner, and knowledge of different types of measurements (regular and formal, regular and informal, and irregular).

Instituting Feedback Systems (15.2)

Once the measurement architecture is implemented, the organization must effectively use it. High-performance leaders *monitor process performance and initiate process improvement efforts as needed.* In other words, they maintain the ability to assess process performance and use measurement results for continual improvement. High-performance leaders understand the relationship between measurement and process improvement.

Feedback is important at the beginning of the process design as a source of input for establishing process goals. Recognizing this, high-performance leaders *design feedback systems* (Harrington, 1991) for their organizations that use meaningful feedback data, feedback loops, and independent auditing and reporting. Knowledge regarding the elements of feedback design and their utilization can support this competency.

Summary

Leaders who enable individuals and teams to recognize, organize, strengthen, and integrate processes can significantly elevate an organization's performance. This chapter outlined competencies related to major process areas that support high-performance leadership at the process level. These competencies may be categorized into several themes regarding the skills and abilities required. First, high-performance leaders acquire knowledge related to process concepts as well as an understanding of tools and options. The leader who acquires this knowledge equips the organization to be responsive to a changing landscape.

Second, high-performance leaders look ahead and anticipate. They look for barriers to processes and their outcomes. They maintain skills related to overcoming those barriers and build them into their planning processes. They keep stakeholders involved in activities at all levels, from the establishment of process goals to process design to process measurement. And they develop and maintain effective lines of communication so that a lack of information does not become a barrier to areas such as process improvement, measurement, or human performance management.

Finally, high-performance leaders keep processes connected to the organization and individual levels. In fact, this skill may be the most critical and distinguishing of the competencies required for high performance at the process level. As Xerox's Paul Allaire stated, "What you're after is congruence among strategic direction, organizational design, staff capabilities, and the processes you use to ensure that people are working together to meet the company's goals" (Garvin, 1995).

References

Davenport, T. H. (1993). *Process innovation.* Boston: Harvard Business School Press.

Galloway, D. (1994). *Mapping work processes.* Milwaukee, WI: ASQC Quality Press.

Garvin, D. (September 1995). Leveraging processes for strategic advantage: A roundtable with Xerox's Galloway, Allaire, USAA's Herres, SmithKline Beecham's Lesch. *Harvard Business Review*, pp. 76–85.

Hackman, J. R., & Wagman, R. (1995). Total quality management: Empirical, conceptual, and practical issues. *Administrative Science Quarterly, 40,* 309–342.

Hammer, M. (1996). *Beyond reengineering: How the process-centered organization is changing our work and our lives.* New York: HarperCollins.

Harrington, H. J. (1987). *The improvement process: How America's leading companies improve quality.* New York: Quality Press (McGraw-Hill Book Company).

Harrington, H. J. (1991). *Business process improvement.* New York: McGraw-Hill.

Hunt, V. D. (1996). *Process mapping.* New York: Wiley.

Juran, J. M. (1992). *Quality by design.* New York: Free Press.

Juran, J. M., & Gryna, F. M. (1993). *Quality planning analysis.* New York: McGraw-Hill.

Lynch, J. J. (June 1996). It's the process (quality management of business processes). *Internal Auditor,* pp. 64–89.

Rummler, G. A., & Brache, A. P. (1995). *Improving performance: How to manage the white space on the organization chart* (2nd ed.). San Francisco: Jossey-Bass.

Chapter 4

▲ High-Performance Leadership at the Individual Level

Lynda S. Wilson
Mary Allyn Boudreaux
Mertis Edwards

The Problem and the Solution. Employees are the foundation of any organization, so effective leaders must have the competencies to lead them to high performance. This chapter describes two competency domains, employee performance and employee potential, and nine competency groups that leaders must master to achieve high performance in an organization. These competencies address Rummler and Brache's (1995) job/performer level of performance.

Human resource managers, industrial psychologists, and human resource development practitioners have long been interested in the study of job satisfaction, motivation, job design, goal setting, and the application of knowledge and skills in the workplace. Rummler and Brache (1995) defined job management as people management and suggested that managers have a tendency to overmanage individuals and undermanage the environment in which they work. This is evidenced by the abundance of literature related to the individual job performer. In the high-performance model, there is a strong link among the three cells of the individual level as well as a connection among goals, design, and management at the individual, process, and organizational level.

Because of the links between these cells, two domains of competencies span all three cells. The first competency domain discussed, employee performance, encompasses the competencies required for goal setting, feedback and coaching, rewards, motivating commitment, and performance assessment. Employee potential, the second competency domain, emphasizes the importance of providing employees with the knowledge, tools, and environment necessary for high performance. These competencies enable leaders to promote employee development through learning opportunities, address barriers within the workplace, optimize employee performance through effective human resource systems, and design jobs that will unleash employee potential.

Employee Performance

Performance is defined as "the avenue by which individuals have an impact on productivity" (Campbell & Campbell, 1990, p. 89). Individuals

▲ **Figure 4.1   Overview of the Individual-Level Competency Domains and Groups**

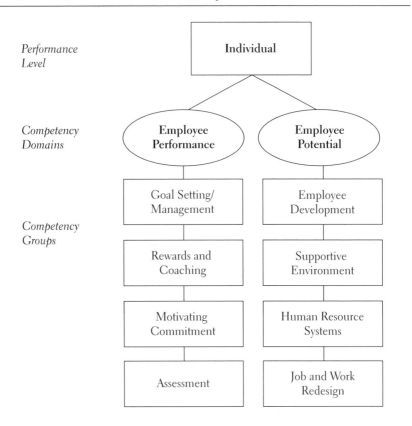

can affect productivity through the efficient execution of job behaviors that accomplish organizational goals while controlling the costs of doing business. Job performers produce outputs and contribute to organizational and process goals. "The quality of outputs is a function of the quality of inputs, performers, consequences, and feedback" (Rummler & Brache, 1995, p. 66). In other words, performance can only be as good as the performer's knowledge, skills, and abilities; understanding of the tasks at hand; awareness of the goals to be achieved; and motivation to perform the job. Several elements of Bolt and Rummler's Performance Chain (1982) reinforce the concept that people perform at higher levels when they have clear goals, the capacity to do the job, and frequent feedback on their performance, and they receive consequences that provide satisfaction.

Goal Setting and Management

Setting performance goals is a widely accepted management practice. Strategies derived from goal-setting theories provide managers with guidelines for setting performance goals (Greenburg & Baron, 1995). To be effective, goals at the individual job performer level must be congruent with the goals of the organization and process levels. Table 4.1 shows the competencies needed to use goal setting effectively.

Ensuring Goal Congruency (16.1)

The purpose of "goal setting is to *integrate individual motives, drives, and needs with organizational goals*" (Curtis, 1994, p. 131). The *linkage of individual performance to organizational productivity (goal alignment)* should be the aim of any goal-setting program (Campbell & Campbell, 1990). In the high-performance workplace, leaders solicit goal commitment by minimizing conflict between organizational and individual goals through strong communication systems, active employee participation, and consistent reinforcement of behaviors that lead to goal attainment.

One antecedent of performance is goal understanding. Performance is enhanced when employees have a *clear picture of what the organization wants them to accomplish* (Campbell & Campbell, 1990). High-performance leaders *communicate organizational goals to gain employee commitment* to the vision of the organization (Bolt & Rummler, 1997; Locke, 1991).

▲ Table 4.1   Goal Setting and Management Competencies

Number	Competency		Subcompetency
16	Goal Setting and Management		
16.1	Ensures goal congruency among individual, process, and organizational goals	16.1a	Integrates individual motives, drives, and needs with organizational goals
		16.1b	Links organizational goals with individual performance
		16.1c	Creates clear picture of performance expectations
		16.1d	Communicates organizational goals to gain employee commitment
16.2	Sets work goals and ensures their attainment	16.2a	Motivates employees through the use of work goals
		16.2b	Teaches employees how to set individual performance goals
		16.2c	Involves employees in goal-setting process
		16.2d	Integrates work goals into human resource management practice
		16.2e	Eliminates barriers to work goal attainment

Setting Work Goals (16.2)

High-performance leaders consider several types of goals. First, they *motivate employees through the setting of performance goals for themselves and their unit* as a whole. Second, they *teach their employees to set individual performance goals.* Goals serve as motivators for performance (Steers & Porter, 1983). Employee commitment to goals should stem from the leader's ability to *involve employees in the goal-setting process* and to energize them into action (Tichy, 1997). High-performance leaders do not underestimate the importance of social factors in goal setting. Group discussion, involvement in goal setting, and sharing information contribute to better employee attitudes and higher levels of performance (Erez & Arad, 1986).

Goals are *integrated into human resource management practices* and are set in three ways: assigned by the leader, set participatively, or self-set (a person can choose a goal). Classical management theories favor leader-assigned goals, humanistic organization theories advocate employee participation in goal setting, and job design advocates favor individual autonomy in the setting of goals (Curtis, 1994). Leaders decide which type of goal-setting practice best fits their organization.

Employees "perform better if goals are defined that are difficult, specific, and attractive" (Katzell & Thompson, 1990, p. 145). Challenging goals motivate individuals to put forth greater effort and persistence and, when they are achieved, leave individuals feeling strong and capable of accomplishing more. Nevertheless, in order to maintain employee morale, goal expectations should not cross "the fine line between being challenging and being insurmountable" (Locke, 1991, p. 78).

High-performance leaders *eliminate any barriers* to goal achievement. Setting goals establishes pathways to positive results and is an important part of human resource management strategies such as job design, training, performance appraisal, participative management, and incentive pay raises (Curtis, 1994). Jobs are designed so that they make the optimum contribution to job goals (Rummler & Brache, 1995). Integrating goal setting into human resource practices makes good sense and is a foundation for a high-performance workplace.

Rewards and Coaching

Effective leaders motivate their followers through feedback, coaching, reward systems, and building employee commitment (Locke, 1991). The integration of these elements is a critical task that high-performance leaders must understand and perform. Leaders have a responsibility to identify rewards that motivate and inspire employees and to develop fair and equitable programs that reward high-performance behavior. The benefits of rewards are best realized when they are aligned with both the culture of the organization and the needs of the employees. The use of feedback and coaching in performance management provides employees with information that will help them reach their full potential. Table 4.2 outlines the reward and coaching competencies that high-performance leaders need.

Creating Effective Reward Systems (17.1)

Leaders use organizational incentives and rewards programs to intensify workers' motivation (Katzell & Thompson, 1990). Once *incentives and rewards are identified*, those most valued by employees are incorporated into a reward program. High-performance leaders *link effort, performance, and valued rewards* so that work is structured to promote personal growth, recognize individual accomplishments, and foster cooperation (Hackman & Wageman, 1995).

Equity theory is concerned with an employee's perception of his or her compensation when compared to others within the organization. High-performance leaders *administer recognition and reward systems fairly and equitably* because employees expect that their compensation (pay, fringe benefits, and bonuses) will be based on the contributions they make (amount of time worked, effort expended, production, and qualifications brought to the job) (Steers & Porter, 1983). Individuals who perceive inequity seek to rectify the situation, and negative behavioral responses may occur, including slacking off on the job, arriving at work late, leaving early, taking longer breaks, doing less work, lowering work standards, or quitting (Greenburg & Baron, 1995).

As the workplace changes, high-performance leaders are responsible for *ensuring that compensation programs provide the best fit between organization and employee goals*. As employees assert more control over their own careers, financial incentives will become increasingly important (Korman, 1999). Also, since high-performance work teams are found in many organizations, reward system design takes into account whether work is done as an individual or as part of a team. When teams are used,

▲ Table 4.2 Reward and Coaching Competencies

Number	Competency		Subcompetency
17	Rewards and Coaching		
17.1	Creates effective reward systems	17.1a	Identifies incentives and rewards that have value for employees
		17.1b	Links effort, performance, and valued rewards
		17.1c	Administers recognition and reward system fairly and equitably
		17.1d	Ensures that compensation program provides for the best fit between the organization and employee goals
17.2	Provides relevant, immediate, frequent feedback	17.2a	Assesses employee performance against goals
		17.2b	Communicates to employees their level of job performance
		17.2c	Provides climate for constructive communication
17.3	Enhances performance through coaching	17.3a	Develops and implements a process for coaching employees
		17.3b	Guides employee efforts to improve performance
		17.3c	Recognizes performance improvement

rewards are administered contingent on the performance of the team as a whole (Hackman & Oldham, 1980).

Providing Feedback to Employees (17.2)

One way that goals regulate performance is through feedback. First, high-performance leaders *assess individual performance against organizational goals* (Curtis, 1994; Locke, 1991). Careful performance measurement is required, and systems are employed that assess individual behavior as objectively as possible. "This measurement should be based on the achievement of key performance objectives and should be formalized so that employees receive regular feedback" (Locke, 1991, p. 82).

High-performance leaders then *communicate to employees their level of job performance*, including whether their work has improved, remained constant, or deteriorated (Hackman & Oldham, 1980). Feedback is most effective when it occurs as the job is being performed. "Feedback provided by the job itself is more immediate and private [and] can increase a worker's feeling of personal control over their work" (Hackman, 1977, p. 250). Open feedback channels contribute to the experienced meaningfulness of a job and, along with the knowledge of results that occur, help create critical psychological states that lead to personal and work outcomes (Fried & Farris, 1987; Hackman & Oldham, 1980; Johns, Xie, & Fang, 1992).

Feedback works more effectively when leaders *provide a climate that is conducive to constructive communication*. "Clear, timely, blunt feedback is the most effective device for improving complex performance" (Bassett, 1994, p. 63). Direct feedback leads to reduced absenteeism, improved psychological and attitudinal outcomes, and improved performance.

Enhancing Performance Through Coaching (17.3)

Coaching is a process that high-performance leaders use to solve performance problems and redirect employee behavior (Fournies, 1987). High-performance leaders understand the concept of coaching and how it assists employees in carrying out their tasks effectively. *Development and implementation of the coaching process* involves the analysis of employee performance as well as encouragement and *guidance for improved performance*. Leaders who are proficient in coaching are patient and do not expect immediate results (Yukl, 1998). When positive performance improvement occurs, leaders *recognize and reinforce that behavior* as soon as possible to increase its influence (Fournies, 1987; Yukl, 1998).

Motivating Commitment

Motivation is defined as "the set of processes that arouse, direct, and maintain behavior toward reaching some goal" (Greenburg & Baron, 1995, p. 142) and is concerned with the choices people make and the direction their behavior takes to fulfill these choices. Motivation has been described as the set of internal and external forces that initiate and determine the form, direction, intensity, and duration of work-related behavior (Ambrose & Kulik, 1999). Theories of motivation and rewards include need, reinforcement, and expectancy theories. Need theory proposes that satisfying human needs is an important part of motivating behavior on the job. Reinforcement theory asserts that effective performance should be positively reinforced so that it is maintained (Steers & Porter, 1983). Expectancy theory asserts that motivation is based on people's belief about the probability that effort will lead to performance and performance will lead to valued rewards (Steers & Porter, 1983). High-performance leaders use motivation to build employee commitment because individual commitment to perform and the persistence of effort over the long term are critical behaviors in a high-performance workplace (Campbell & Campbell, 1990).

Using Motivation Theory to Build Commitment (18.1)

To achieve maximum employee commitment while maintaining high levels of worker satisfaction, an organization must "pay and promote fairly, communicate openly and honestly, offer interesting, meaningful work, select, train and place workers skillfully, provide work schedules that fit emerging lifestyles and elicit workers 'best efforts'" (Bassett, 1994, p. 67). Leaders can promote job satisfaction as well as the mission of the organization by *selecting the appropriate method of motivation.*

High-performance leaders use their knowledge of motivational theories to select the most appropriate method for increasing employee motivation and thus job satisfaction. These methods are *integrated into daily performance management practices.* Traditional approaches for promoting

▲ Table 4.3 Motivating Commitment Competencies

Number	Competency		Subcompetency
Motivating Commitment			
18.1	Uses motivational theories to strengthen employee commitment to the organization	18.1a	Selects the appropriate method to motivate individuals
		18.1b	Integrates motivational theory into daily performance management
		18.1c	Acknowledges effect of workforce trends on employee commitment to the organization
18.2	Designs interesting and meaningful jobs that improve worker satisfaction and ensure achievement of organizational goals	18.2a	Designs jobs that ensure the best fit between employees' knowledge, skills, and abilities and their need for autonomy, feedback, personal growth, and meaningfulness of work
		18.2b	Determines individual need for growth and designs work accordingly
18.3	Employs participative management strategies aimed at improving job satisfaction	18.3a	Provides employees with opportunities to participate in managerial processes
		18.3b	Gains commitment throughout the organization for employee involvement
		18.3c	Aligns participative management with human resource policies

employee satisfaction include improved selection, placement, and training programs; changes in supervisory practices; the addition of workplace amenities; and the use of incentives (Yukl, 1989).

Three trends have created a different world of work and have changed the way high-performance leaders look at motivation (Korman, 1999). The first trend, downsizing of the workforce, causes anxiety and affects employee motivation. The second trend, the emergence of work-family conflict, is characterized by women in the workforce, dual-career couples, and single-parent families. The third trend is the increased use of contingent employees as well as the outsourcing of traditional job functions. High-performance leaders *acknowledge and understand the effect that workforce trends have on employee commitment to the organization* and adjust motivational practices accordingly.

Designing Interesting and Meaningful Jobs (18.2)

High-performance leaders *design jobs that ensure the best fit between employees' knowledge, skills, and abilities and their need for autonomy, feedback, personal growth, and meaningfulness of work.* If the goal is to make jobs attractive, interesting, and satisfying, then job enrichment programs may be the best solution (Katzell & Thompson, 1990). A common model for job enrichment, the Job Characteristics Model, is based on behavioral and systems theory and takes into account individual differences in the way employees perform their job (Hackman & Oldham, 1980). The question for leaders to ask is, "How can work be structured so that it is performed effectively and, at the same time, jobholders find the work personally rewarding and satisfying?" (p. 71).

The Job Characteristics Model associates certain job characteristics (autonomy, feedback, skill variety, skill identity, and task significance) with critical psychological states necessary for the development of internal motivation, such as experienced meaningfulness of work, responsibility for work outcomes, and knowledge of the results of work. The effects of job characteristics on performance will vary based on situational or individual differences (Fried & Ferris, 1987). High-performance leaders *determine the individual's need for growth in his or her job and redesign work accordingly.* The knowledge and skills of the individual as well as the work context may affect the motivating potential of a job (Fried & Ferris, 1987; Hackman & Oldham, 1980).

When jobs are enriched, leaders expect increased internal work motivation and growth satisfaction, higher-quality work performance, high job satisfaction and work effectiveness, and decreased absenteeism and turnover (Fried & Ferris, 1987). "Job enrichment in actual work situations can yield significant improvements in performance" (Berlinger, Glick, & Rogers, 1990, p. 237).

Employing Participative Management Strategies (18.3)

Participative management, another strategy to promote job satisfaction, *"provides employees with opportunities to participate actively in managerial processes* (planning, goal setting, problem solving and decision making) affecting job-related matters" (Banas, 1990, p. 406). Worker participation increases when high-performance leaders *gain commitment throughout all levels of the organization for employee involvement* (Klein, Smith-Major, & Ralls, 1999). Participation practices are *aligned with human resource policies* relevant to training, rewards, and placement. When combined with an employee involvement partnership, they increase job satisfaction through improved production and work environments.

Assessment

Management practice at the individual level is concerned with the linkage between the individual job performer and the design of the job. While leaders need to be aware of organizational and process assessment practices, the focus here is the identification of competencies needed to accomplish assessment at the individual and job levels (see Table 4.4).

Linking Behavior with Organizational Goals (19.1)

Assessment as part of performance management involves *evaluation of the individual, the job, the process, and the desired organizational results.* To assess performance at the individual level, high-performance leaders link individual behavior with the goals of the organization and its processes (Banks & May, 1999). They *determine whether the job is designed in such a way as to maximize employee performance outcomes* and *assess individuals' knowledge, skills, and abilities* to do their job.

▲ Table 4.4   Assessment Competencies

Number	Competency	Subcompetency	
19	Assessment		
19.1	Links individual behavior with goals of the organization	19.1a	Evaluates individual, job process, and organizational results
		19.1b	Determines if job design maximizes outcomes
		19.1c	Assesses employee knowledge, skills, and attitudes
19.2	Reviews employee performance through a formal appraisal system	19.2a	Reviews employee job performance
		19.2b	Provides appropriate performance intervention
		19.2c	Incorporates performance appraisal into a continuous improvement program
		19.2d	Ensures fairness and objectivity in appraisals

Reviewing Employee Performance (19.2)

Performance appraisal, a systematic *review of individual employee performance on the job*, provides high-performance leaders with information regarding employee skill levels, or lack thereof, and can *provide the foundation for appropriate performance interventions* (Muchinsky, 1993). Information obtained from appraisals assists leaders in making decisions regarding raises, promotions, transfers, discharge, or training interventions.

Performance appraisals, an ongoing component of an overall continuous improvement program, provide valuable feedback regarding individual and organizational performance (Banks & May, 1999). High-performance leaders *ensure that appraisals are performed fairly and objectively.* The efforts to develop an employee evaluation process that has the best interests of the organization and its people must be sustained. "People's promotions, pay, and career development depend on it" (Curtis, 1994, p. 143).

Employee Potential

Maximization of employee potential stems from the organization's commitment to nurture and develop its workforce. The high-performance leader is responsible for enhancing employees' capabilities to perform their jobs through employee development programs. In addition, leaders have to provide an environment that is supportive for performance, ensures that adequate resources are available, and eliminates barriers to performance through the proper design of jobs.

Employee Development

Employee development is the building up or nurturing of individual employees in order to bring out the best in them and help them to reach their highest potential. Programs that promote employee well-being, career development, and the practice of lifelong learning are integral components of a comprehensive employee development program (see Table 4.5).

Providing Opportunities for Continual Learning (20.1)

Learning is an important part of being human and can help individuals change their perceptions of the world and their relationship to it, and extend their capacity to create. This ability to redefine oneself continuously is important in a high-performance workplace, where changes are the norm and employees are expected to adapt to that change (Senge, 1990). Although "the inclination to learn is built in, people also require tools and coaching if they are to express that inclination in their work behavior" (Hackman & Wageman, 1995, p. 330).

There is a need for continual learning in organizations because "people cannot contribute to the aims and aspirations of an organization if they do not know what to do, and they cannot help if they do not know how to do it" (Kouzes & Posner, 1993, p. 54). Leaders continually *develop the capacity of their employees* by *providing an environment conducive to learning.* The leader's role is that of a teacher who helps others learn and develop new skills by fostering an environment that supports ongoing experiential learning and maturation (Kouzes & Posner, 1993; Senge, 1990; Tichy, 1997).

Enhancing Employee Well-Being (20.2)

High-performance leaders *recognize and respond to the personal needs of their employees* by tracking career trends and work and other life issues. Alternative work arrangements *accommodate employee lifestyle differences* and allow for flexible work schedules and work-at-home programs (Cummings & Worley, 1997). However, "work/life issues aren't just about dependent care and flexible schedules." Issues related to the work itself and workplace stress are also important (Caudron, 1998, p. 22). High-performance leaders *redesign jobs to reduce unnecessary workplace stress.*

Employers can *offer programs to address the quality of employee work-life*, which includes "the task, the physical work environment, the social environment within the organization, the administrative system, and the relationship between life on and off of the job" (Cunningham & Eberle, 1990, p. 57). Programs such as diversity interventions address workplace issues and compel employees to evaluate and appreciate differences in age, gender, disabilities, cultural values, and sexual orientation. Family-leave programs assist employees in meeting health care, child care, and maternity and paternity leave needs. Mobility, physical access, job security, and workplace safety accommodations are addressed. Wellness, stress management programs, and employee assistance programs offered at many organizations assist with a variety of employee welfare issues.

▲ Table 4.5   Employee Development Competencies

Number	Competency		Subcompetency
20	Employee Development		
20.1	Provides opportunity for continual learning	20.1a	Develops capacity of employees
		20.1b	Provides an environment conducive to learning
20.2	Enhances employee well-being through programs and activities	20.2a	Recognizes and responds to personal needs of employees
		20.2b	Accommodates employee lifestyle differences
		20.2c	Redesigns jobs to reduce unnecessary work and workplace stress
		20.2d	Offers programs that address the quality of employee work life
20.3	Develops career management programs	20.3a	Assists employees in identifying their skills, interests, and motivations for career growth
		20.3b	Prepares employees for job of the future with organization's career development needs
		20.3c	Implements career progression programs
		20.3d	Solicits employee input into his or her career planning process
		20.3e	Identifies and communicates opportunities and standards for promotion

20.4	Develops employee knowledge, skills, and attitudes through training initiatives	20.4a	Identifies competencies for successful job performance
		20.4b	Determines critical training needs
		20.4c	Develops and implements training interventions
		20.4d	Ensures transfer of training
		20.4e	Evaluates effectiveness of training

Developing Career Management Programs (20.3)

High-performance leaders act as assessor, information provider, referral agent, guide, teacher, and developer of the career development program (Knowdell, 1996). They *assist employees in identifying their skills, interests, and motivation for career growth* and inform them of options for career movement. A career development program *prepares employees for jobs of the future,* where there will be less opportunity for upward mobility and more emphasis on expanded skills and competencies in a horizontal career path (McLagan, 1990). High-performance leaders *implement career progression programs* that develop the workforce through challenging work, the sequencing of job assignments, and job rotation plans to advance the knowledge, skills, and abilities of their employees (Kraiger, 1999).

The responsibility for career development is an individual responsibility as well. The high-performance leader therefore *solicits employee input into the career planning process* so that employees become active participants in their own professional growth and development. Because of the fundamental changes in the workplace and how people perform their jobs, individuals increasingly will take more control over their own career management. Self-guided career management programs assist individuals to make decisions about their careers and adapt to the temporary nature of work settings by helping them develop skills and prepare for inevitable changes (Korman, 1999).

The organization's role is primarily one of providing information and resources where high-performance leaders act as consultants and career development specialists. Leaders *identify and communicate opportunities and standards for advancement* so that employees can take full advantage of professional growth opportunities (Bassett, 1994).

Developing Employees Through Training (20.4)

High-performance leaders *identify competencies necessary for the successful performance of the job* and use this information to *determine critical training needs* that address performance gaps and facilitate employee transition from novice to expert. These leaders also *develop and implement training interventions* based on research and needs assessment activities that identify the knowledge, skills, and attitudes necessary for job performance (Campbell & Campbell, 1990).

Training, the process through which people systematically acquire and improve the skills and knowledge needed for improved job performance, takes many forms (Greenburg & Baron, 1995). Apprenticeship programs in which classroom instruction is combined with on-the-job instruction are growing in popularity, as are executive training programs, where companies systematically seek to develop the skills of their top managers. Some companies have developed their own corporate universities devoted to handling training needs on a full-time basis.

No one approach to training is ideal, and the best programs often use many different approaches that incorporate different learning principles. For training to be effective, learning must be applied on the job, so the more closely a program matches the demands and conditions of a job, the more effective it will be. High-performance leaders *ensure transfer of training* by encouraging employees to apply their newly learned skills on the job. They *evaluate the effectiveness of training programs* by not only looking at whether the employee can apply new skills to the job, but also whether the skills benefit the organization as a whole.

Supportive Environment

Work environments can either contribute to organizational performance or detract from it. Employees need resources and an atmosphere conducive to high performance. Therefore, a high-performance leader must endorse creating a work environment that promotes safety, provides adequate work resources, and removes barriers to achieving high performance (see Table 4.6).

Managing Resources (21.1)

Leaders effectively manage resources within their control so that the desired goals of the organizations can be met. It is first necessary to *determine which resources can optimize job performance*. Resources include all of the tangible and intangible things required for an organization to meet its objectives: facilities and equipment, energy, power and other utilities, materials and supplies, human resources, information and data, and money or capital (Bittel, 1989). The goal of any organization is to maximize profits and minimize resource allocation. At the individual level, it is the leader's responsibility to *manage resources within the limitations*

▲ Table 4.6 Supportive Environment Competencies

Number	Competency		Subcompetency
21	Supportive environment		
21.1	Manages resources (time, money, data, equipment, manpower) of work unit to meet organizational goals	21.1a	Determines which resources optimize performance
		21.1b	Manages resources within limits imposed by organization
21.2	Provides a safe and ergonomically sound work environment	21.2a	Designs work environment to minimize risk of injury
		21.2b	Applies ergonomic principles to the work area
		21.2c	Evaluates the cost of workplace injury on quality and productivity
21.3	Eliminates barriers to performance	21.3a	Removes performance constraints in the workplace
		21.3b	Provides supportive organizational context
		21.3c	Evaluates organizational systems (technology, personnel, and control) effect on job performance

imposed by the organization and ensure that jobs are designed to capitalize on the use of these resources.

Providing a Safe and Ergonomically Sound Work Environment (21.2)

One major source of resource depletion is workplace accidents. "Approximately 200,000 American workers suffer from ergonomic-related ailments" (Attaran, 1996, p. 19). Another 60 to 120 million workers are considered at risk for these ailments. High-performance leaders therefore *design the work environment to minimize the risk of injury* while providing employees with the tools and information needed to be productive (Attaran, 1996; Rummler & Brache, 1990).

In the high-performance workplace, leaders *apply ergonomic principles to the work area*: layout, work procedures and methods, selection of proper work tools and equipment, and worker training (Attaran, 1996). Repetitive motion, hand force, posture, workplace, contact stress, vibration, materials handling, and the physical environment (noise, temperature, and lighting) are just a few of the risk factors for injury in the workplace (Hansen & Sysar, 1997). To reduce the costs of workplace injury, accepted principles of ergonomic management are incorporated into the design of new systems, the evaluation of existing facilities, and any recommendations for improvement.

The costs of not doing so are too high to ignore. Over $40 billion is spent each year in the United States on workplace injuries (Attaran, 1996). High-performance leaders *evaluate the cost of workplace injuries and their effects on lost quality and productivity.*

Eliminating Barriers to Performance (21.3)

An effective leader must *remove all performance constraints in the workplace* through the reorganization of work, the modification of technology, the provision of resources, and the removal of physical constraints (Yukl, 1989). High-performance leaders *provide a supportive organizational context*, which includes managerial support (resources, information, and encouragement) (Campion, 1988).

Physical barriers or performance constraints in the workplace are not the only impediments to high performance. Operating systems within an organization can place barriers in the way of employee productivity and job enrichment. High-performance leaders *evaluate technology, personnel and supervisory systems, and control systems* to identify any impediments to job performance (Cummings & Worley, 1997).

Human Resource Systems

High-performance leaders embrace a human resource system that values strategic selection and placement practices. Linking the right employee to the right job has enormous potential to improve performance. In today's workplace, recruiting and retaining high-performing individuals adds value to an organization. Table 4.7 outlines the competencies that high-performance leaders need in this area.

Adhering to Policies (22.1)

High-performance leaders adhere to comprehensive policies and procedures that comply with federal, state, and local regulations by *interpreting laws as they relate to the workplace*. Many regulations that govern issues such as labor, the environment, and intellectual property have an impact on the organization, even at the individual level. Leaders are expected to *understand the laws that have a direct effect on the work unit* and its employees and *ensure that the organization complies with applicable laws and regulations* to minimize liability.

High-performance leaders *link human resource policies and procedures with job activities*. Then leaders must *communicate established policies* to employees. Communication channels can be used that lead to successful integration of these policies into daily work activities. High-performance leaders continually *evaluate whether the organization's policies and procedures help or hinder performance* (Rummler & Brache, 1995).

Recruitment, Selection, and Placement (22.2)

The high-performance leader *develops commitment to the organization through the recruitment process* and creates successful organizations by *choosing individuals whose values closely match those of the organization* (Greenburg & Baron, 1995). Through selection and placement strategies, high-performance leaders *identify and develop future leaders* who want to "develop themselves and others" (Tichy, 1997, p. 285).

▲ Table 4.7 Human Resource Systems Competencies

Number	Competency		Subcompetency
22	Human Resource Systems		
22.1	Adheres to policies, procedures, and regulations of federal, state, and local governments	22.1a	Interprets government policies as they relate to the workplace and ensures compliance
		22.1b	Understands laws that affect the work unit and ensure organizational compliance
		22.1c	Links policies and procedures with job activities and communicates to employees
		22.1d	Evaluates the effect of policies and procedures on performance
22.2	Optimizes job performance through recruitment, selection, and placement of employees	22.2a	Develops employee commitment through recruitment practices
		22.2b	Chooses employees with values congruent with the organization
		22.2c	Uses selection and placement strategies to identify and develop future leaders
		22.2d	Places employees based on fit between job design and employee competencies

High-performance leaders *place employees in the right position based on the fit between the design of the job and employee competencies.* Flexible job models provide a mechanism for the evaluation of jobs and the competencies needed to perform them (McLagan, 1990). These models provide a focus for needs analysis, training design and development, and job design. Job menus are key components of flexible job design and provide answers to the questions, "What is to be produced?" and, "What must be mastered?" (p. 370). The strategic organizational plan as well as process requirements are considered.

Job and Work Redesign

Motivational approaches to job design seek to optimize employee job satisfaction and work enrichment. Three other approaches are mechanistic, biological, and perceptual/motor (Campion, 1988). The mechanistic approach, oriented to "human resource efficiency and flexibility" (p. 467), reflects classic industrial engineering strategies. The biological approach focuses on ergonomic requirements and the workplace environment. Finally, the perceptual/motor approach relates to "human mental capabilities and limitations" (p. 468), especially as they relate to stress, fatigue, and mental overload. High-performance leaders incorporate these approaches into their job design practices.

Recognizing When Job Redesign Is Needed (23.1)

Work redesign approaches "seek to improve an organization's coordination, productivity, and overall product quality as well as to respond to employees' needs for learning, challenge, variety, increased responsibility, and achievement" (Cunningham & Eberle, 1990). Activities involve "alteration of specific jobs with the intent of improving both productivity and the quality of employee work experiences" (Hackman & Lee, 1979, p. 1). Work redesign efforts directly change behavior and alter the relationship between the individual and what he or she does on the job.

Jobs must be structured so individuals can achieve personal, process, and organization goals. If jobs are not so structured, then high-performance leaders *determine whether jobs can benefit from redesign efforts.* Hackman and Oldham (1980) suggest six questions for *assessing the need and/or feasibility for work redesign* (p. 128):

- Is there a problem or exploitable opportunity?
- Does the problem or opportunity centrally involve employee motivation, satisfaction or work effectiveness?
- Might the design of the work be responsible for observed problems?
- What aspects of the job most need improvement?
- How ready are the employees for change?
- How hospitable are organizational systems to needed changes?

Job redesign is time-consuming to plan, execute, and monitor (it can take months or even years) and should be held to high standards of evaluation (Muchinsky, 1993). High-performance leaders *consider the effects of work redesign on the entire work system and the organization.* Changes in job design are not likely to improve performance unless new procedures are at least as efficient as old ones (Katzell & Thompson, 1990).

It is important to *consider the alignment of job content with process requirements and organizational goals* (Campbell & Campbell, 1990; Rummler & Brache, 1995). "Job design must be flexible, provide appropriate guidance for decision-making under uncertainty and reflect strategies and future needs of the business" (McLagan, 1990, p. 369). It is the process of assigning outputs for a job based on an organization's current needs as well as those identified for the future success of the organization. Outputs are also assigned to a job based on the current "capability, motivation and development priorities" (p. 369) of the individual and others in the organization or work team.

Determining Appropriateness of Group Job Design (23.2)

The leader determines whether redesigned work should be performed by individuals or in work groups or teams based on organization and process requirements. The high-performance leader *assesses the organizational climate* to *determine whether it is conducive to group work* and *whether the organizational system can accommodate changes needed for group work* (Hackman & Oldham, 1980). In some circumstances, groups perform tasks better than individuals because the job is done more quickly and errors are identified and corrected more efficiently as the task is done. When tough decisions are necessary or the job involves critical work, groups such as task forces are often formed because people involved in the process are more likely to accept the decisions.

▲ **Table 4.8 Job Design and Work Redesign Competencies**

Number	Competency		Subcompetency
23	Job and Work Redesign Competencies		
23.1	Recognizes when job redesign is needed to support organizational goals and processes	23.1a	Determines whether jobs can benefit from redesign efforts
		23.1b	Assesses need and/or feasibility of work redesign
		23.1c	Considers the effects of work redesign on the work system and the organization
		23.1d	Aligns job content with process requirements and organizational goals
23.2	Determines when group job design is more appropriate than individual job design	23.2a	Assesses organizational climate
		23.2b	Evaluates organizational systems so as to accommodate group work
		23.2c	Determines the feasibility of creating a work group
		23.2d	Determines whether work groups can be managed and supported

23.3	Uses knowledge of group design to form groups (selection and size) and define individual task design	23.3a	Applies group dynamic and interpersonal process principles to the management of work teams
		23.3b	Provides a supportive organizational context
		23.3c	Monitors the design of the group
		23.3d	Provides training, technical consultation, and task clarification

Groups should be used only when they appear to offer substantial advantages over enriched individual jobs (Hackman & Oldham, 1980). Thus, high-performance leaders *determine the feasibility of creating a work group* given the nature of the task and its organizational context. And if a group is formed, this leader *determines if it can be managed and supported appropriately.*

Forming Work Groups (23.3)

The management of work teams requires high-performance leaders to *apply group dynamics and interpersonal principles* as well as make adjustments to management styles (Hackman & Oldham, 1980). To ensure work team effectiveness, leaders *provide a supportive organizational context* in which to work. The size and composition of the group and the selection of group members are also considerations (Campion, Popper, & Medsker, 1996). Rewards and performance objectives tailored to the task at hand take into account the performance of the group as a whole. Goals are set collaboratively, and feedback is provided to the group. High-performance leaders take steps to coordinate the group's effort and develop commitment among group members to the task.

The group thus becomes adept at "handling social and interpersonal issues, managing technical and administrative matters and analyzing economic trade-offs" (Hackman & Oldham, 1980, p. 211). High-performance leaders continuously *monitor the design of the group* and the organizational context so that problems can be identified and changes made in order to increase the group's performance. The leader also acts as a consultant, *providing training, technical consultation, and task clarification* until the group is capable of self-management.

Summary

There is a tendency for today's organizational leaders to conclude that organizational problems are individual problems. Therefore, they frequently overmanage their employees. This chapter identified competencies that leaders can use to avoid overmanagement and become the high-performance leaders of the future.

High-performance leaders are concerned with maximizing individual employee performance and potential. The leader affects productivity through goal setting, motivation, and assessment. Goals provide direction to both the leader and employees, and motivation builds commitment to the organization. Assessment of performance provides a yardstick for individual and organizational achievement.

To maximize employee potential, high-performance leaders develop employees through learning opportunities and career development activities. When employees have a supportive work environment, they can develop professionally and personally. Employee potential is maximized if jobs are well designed and policies and procedures support job activities.

References

Ambrose, M. L., & Kulik, C. T. (1999). Old friends, new faces: Motivation research in the 1990s. *Journal of Management, 25*(3), 231–292.

Attaran, M. (1996). Adopting an integrated approach to ergonomics implementation. *IIE Solutions, 26*(6), 19–23.

Banas, P. A. (1990). Employee involvement: A sustained labor/management initiative at the Ford Motor Company. In J. P. Campbell & R. J. Campbell (Eds.), *Productivity in organizations: New perspectives from industrial and organizational psychology* (pp. 388–416). San Francisco: Jossey-Bass.

Banks, C. G., & May, K. E. (1999). Performance management: The real glue in organizations. In A. I. Kraut & A. K. Korman (Eds.), *Evolving practices in human resource management* (pp. 118–145). San Francisco: Jossey-Bass.

Bassett, G. (1994, May–June). The case against job satisfaction. *Business Horizons*, 61–68.

Berlinger, L. R., Glick, W. H., & Rodgers, R. C. (1990). Job enrichment and performance improvement. In J. P. Campbell & R. J. Campbell (Eds.), *Productivity in organizations: New perspectives from industrial and organizational psychology* (pp. 219–254). San Francisco: Jossey-Bass.

Bittel, L. R. (1989). *The McGraw-Hill 36–hour management course.* New York: McGraw-Hill.

Bolt, J. F., & Rummler, G. A. (1982). How to close the performance gap. *Management Review, 71*(1) 38–44.

Campbell, J. P., & Campbell, R. J. (1990). Industrial-organization psychology and productivity: The goodness of fit. In J. P. Campbell & R. J. Campbell (Eds.), *Productivity in organizations: New perspectives from industrial and organizational psychology* (pp. 82–93). San Francisco: Jossey-Bass.

Campion, M. A. (1988). Interdisciplinary approaches to job design: A constructive replication with extensions. *Journal of Applied Psychology, 73*(3), 467–481.

Campion, M. A., Popper, E. M., & Medsker, G. I. (1996). Relations between work team characteristics and effectiveness: A replication and extension. *Personnel Psychology, 49*(2), 429–453.

Caudron, S. (1998). On the contrary, job stress is in job design. *Workforce, 77*(9), 21–24.

Cummings, T. G., & Worley, C. (1997). *Organizational development and change* (6th ed.). Cincinnati, OH: South-Western College Publishing.

Cunningham, J. B., & Eberle, T. (1990). A guide to job enrichment and redesign. *Personnel, 67*(2), 56–62.

Curtis, K. (1994). *From management goal setting to organizational results: Transforming strategies into action.* Westport, CT: Quorum Books.

Erez, M., & Arad, R. (1986). Participative goal setting: Social, motivational, and cognitive factors. *Journal of Applied Psychology, 71*(4), 591–597.

Fournies, F. F. (1987). *Coaching for improved work performance.* New York: McGraw-Hill.

Fried, Y., & Ferris, G. R. (1987). The validity of the job characteristics model: A review and meta-analysis. *Personnel Psychology, 40*, 287–322.

Greenburg, J., & Baron, R. (1995). *Behavior in organizations.* Englewood Cliffs, NJ: Prentice Hall.

Hackman, J. R. (1977). Designing work for individuals and for groups. In J. R. Hackman, E. E. Lawler III, & L. W. Porter (Eds.), *Perspectives on behavior in organizations* (pp. 242–256). New York: McGraw-Hill.

Hackman, J. R., & Lee, M. D. (1979). *Redesigning work: A strategy for change.* Scarsdale, NY: Work in America Institute, Inc.

Hackman, J. R., & Oldham, G. R. (1980). *Work redesign.* Reading, MA: Addison-Wesley.

Hackman, J. R., & Wageman, J. R. (1995). Total quality management: Empirical, conceptual, and practical issues. *Administrative Science Quarterly, 40*, 309–342.

Hansen, M. D., & Sysar, D. S. (1997). Making the right moves: Implementing effective ergonomics management. *Risk Management, 44*(2), 50–54.

Johns, G., Xie, J. L., & Fang, Y. (1992). Mediating and moderating effects in job design. *Journal of Management, 18*(4), 657–676.

Katzell, R. A., & Thompson, D. E. (1990). Work motivation: Theory and practice. *American Psychologist, 42*(2), 144–153.

Klein, K. J., Smith-Major, V. L., & Ralls, R. W. (1999). Worker participation: Current promise, future prospects. In A. I. Kraut & A. K. Korman (Eds.), *Evolving practices in human resource management* (pp. 226–248). San Francisco: Jossey-Bass.

Knowdell, R. L. (1996). *Building a career development program: Nine steps for effective implementation.* Palo Alto, CA: Davies-Black Publishing.

Korman, A. K. (1999). Motivation, commitment, and the "new contracts" between employers and employees. In A. I. Kraut & A. K. Korman (Eds.), *Evolving practices in human resource management* (pp. 23–40). San Francisco: Jossey-Bass.

Kouzes, J. M., & Posner, B. Z. (1993). *Credibility: How leaders gain and lose it, why people demand it.* San Francisco: Jossey-Bass.

Kraiger, K. (1999). Performance and employee development. In D. R. Ilgen & E. D. Pulakos (Eds.), *The changing nature of performance: Implications for staffing, motivation, and development* (pp. 366–396). San Francisco: Jossey-Bass.

Locke, E. (1991). *The essence of leadership: Four keys to leading successfully.* San Francisco: New Lexington Press.

Muchinsky, P. M. (1993). *Psychology applied to work* (4th ed.). Pacific Grove, CA: Brooks/Cole.

Rummler, G., & Brache, A. (1995). *Improving performance: How to manage the white space on the organizational chart* (2nd ed.). San Francisco: Jossey-Bass.

Senge, P. (1990). *The fifth discipline.* New York: Doubleday.

Steers, M., & Porter, L. W. (1983). *Motivation and work behavior* (3rd ed.). New York: McGraw-Hill.

Tichy, N. M. (1997). *The leadership engine.* New York: HarperBusiness.

Yukl, G. A. (1989). Managerial leadership: A review of theory and research. *Journal of Management, 15*(2), 251–289.

Yukl, G. A. (1998). *Leadership in organizations.* Englewood Cliffs, NJ: Prentice Hall.

Chapter 5

▲ Implementing Performance-Based Leadership Development

Elwood F. Holton III
Sharon S. Naquin

The Problem and the Solution. The previous chapters have developed a new performance-based competency model of leadership development. As a generic model, it is applicable to virtually any organization. If you are in charge of leadership development, you may be asking yourself, "How do I change our leadership development process to fit this model?" This chapter provides guidance for implementing the model.

This chapter is written from the point of view of an HRD director or manager who wants to implement the model presented in the previous chapters. The power of the model is that it is a generic performance-based leadership competency model that can be used to build leadership development efforts in any organization. Nevertheless, few generic models fit every organization, so most organizations will have to customize it to fit their needs. Some organizations will simply have to localize the language; others will need to fit it to their culture. All will need to make decisions about what specific strategies and training will be used to build the competencies.

For some organizations, moving to the performance-based leadership development model will constitute a substantial change. Our assumption is that most organizations have some type of leadership development in place, even if it is quite basic. Thus, our bias is that implementing performance-based leadership is best viewed through an organizational change lens.

The Change Process

Figure 5.1 displays the leadership development system change process recommended to guide implementation of the model. The process begins with an organization's recognition that more effective leadership and, by extension, leadership development is needed to sustain or achieve performance targets. Leadership development increasingly is

▲ **Figure 5.1   Leadership Development System Change Process**

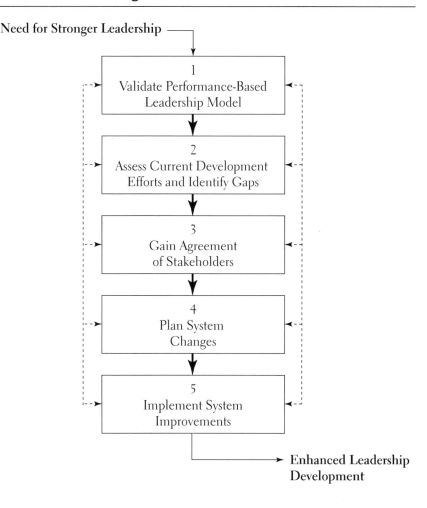

being recognized as a strategic issue in organizations (Conger & Benjamin, 1999). The power of performance-based leadership development is most likely to be realized when leadership is recognized as a key variable influencing organizational goal achievement.

The change process is based on action research approaches to organizational change (Cummings & Worley, 1997). Action research has several distinguishing features that make it particularly well suited for this change process (as well as many others). First, it is a collaborative process that engages those who are affected by the change in joint diagnosis, planning, and implementation. Second, it is an iterative process whereby organizational members continually implement, reassess, and fine-tune change initiatives. Third, by avoiding an "expert" model of change, greater buy-in from key stakeholders is obtained through their participation in the process. Fourth, it is widely used in organizational change initiatives.

A key limitation of action research methodologies is that they may be less potent when transformational change is needed. Sometimes widespread agreement about leadership development system change is not feasible because of resistance from leaders entrenched in established ways of leading. In those cases, the action research process may be best restricted to high-performing leaders who then work to overcome resistance from other leaders in the organization.

Step 1: Validating the Performance-Based Leadership Model

The question at this step is, "Is the model complete and accurate for our organization?" A variety of strategies are used to validate competency models. Many employ survey techniques to assess the fit of the competencies across a broad cross-section of leaders. Although these techniques have their place, we recommend a different strategy that uses only high-performing leaders as the validation group. The logic is simple: organizations should validate the competencies using only high-performing leaders whom they would like to develop more of in the future. This is likely to be only a small group. The result will be validation of the competencies needed by best performers, not just the average performer.

The initial step in the process requires the selection of a group of subject matter experts (SMEs) to serve as the development planning team. These experts should generally represent a cross-section of leaders who perform at the level typical of what is desired as an outcome of the leadership development programs and content experts who can contribute expertise in specific subject areas.

The first task for the development team is to validate the competencies contained in this model. The outcome of this task should be general agreement by high-performing leaders that the model, or some variation of it, represents the target competencies for leaders in the organization. The task is not to determine whether the model is descriptive of a current leadership in the organization but rather whether the model is descriptive of the way leadership should be in the future. Modifications to the model should be made with caution, because the model is deeply rooted in theory and research. Generally modifications are most likely to occur at the subcompetency level, not at the competency or competency group levels. The validation process itself may be conducted in an informal, consensus-building approach or in a more formal group process, such as the nominal group technique.

Step 2: Assessing Current Development Efforts and Identifying Gaps

The next step is to compare competencies developed by the existing programs to those in the new competency model. First, the learning objectives for the existing programs should be mapped to competencies in this model. Then the competencies for which new programs must be developed can be easily identified. In addition, existing programs can be placed into the larger theoretical framework of this model. Any gaps identified in existing programs become the driver for curriculum development efforts.

Step 3: Gaining Agreement of Stakeholders

The strong support of existing leaders, particularly high-performing ones and those in senior management positions, is vitally important to leadership development efforts. The third step then is to gain the agreement of important organizational stakeholders on an action plan for program development. This step requires caution because changes in the leadership development program may well threaten some existing leaders, resulting in resistance and naysaying. Nonetheless, important stakeholders will have to be convinced that the new competency model should be implemented. Fortunately, the performance foundation for this model should make it an easier sell, particularly to senior management.

Step 4: Planning System Changes

The process of moving from this model to the curriculum development phase is relatively systematic.

Conducting an Activity Analysis Meeting

An activity analysis meeting should be conducted with the development planning team formed in Step One to break each competency and sub-competency into lower-level activity statements. Activity analysis is defined as the analysis of work activities and is used when job functions are not task oriented, such as in management jobs. It is similar to task analysis, but activities are broader and better suited to leadership curriculum development. The team should be subdivided into small groups, with the number of groups corresponding to the number of competencies to be analyzed. Each group should be assigned to one competency and instructed to define what a high-performing leader would do if he or she were performing the competency at a desired level. In training jargon, the group members are defining the performance objectives for training.

The group members should brainstorm responses and reach consensus on the list of activities. This step is the essence of the meeting and may be quite time-consuming. Ideally, one representative of the group should record the responses on flip-chart paper. When the small groups reassemble into one large group, typically a representative from each group reports the group's list to the larger group. The larger group should be allowed to contribute additional activities or comment on the activities generated by each small group.

Analyzing Activity Analysis Data

The list of activities for each competency should be analyzed for common themes and grouped accordingly. Usually the list can be reduced by some selective clustering, which will facilitate the next step. Then the group is asked, "Would a training program that enables participants to do these activities result in the development of a successful manager for this competency?" If the answer is yes, the group is done. If the answer is no, the group adds activities until they can answer yes.

Conducting a Knowledge, Skills, and Abilities Meeting

The objective of this meeting is to define what it is a successful leader should know in order to perform each of the activity groups that emerged from the activity analysis. In training jargon, they are defining the learning objectives. The groups must be cautioned not to become too detailed in their comments because the purpose is to develop objectives, not detailed teaching guides. Usually it is best to do this with the same group of SMEs used for the activity analysis step. However, it is sometimes useful to change the composition of the group if it will contribute new expertise. Once again, the SMEs should be divided into small groups, with each group assigned to a competency and the corresponding activities identified in the previous activity analysis steps.

The group process proceeds in almost identical manner as the activity analysis meeting. The group members should brainstorm responses and reach consensus on the list. This step, which may take several hours or more to complete, is the heart of this meeting. A representative of the group should write the group's list on flip-chart paper. After the list has been recorded, the small group should be reassembled into one larger group, and each group reports its list to the larger group. The larger group should be allowed sufficient time to contribute additional knowledge, skills, and abilities (KSAs) or comment on the KSA statements generated by each small group. This process should continue until all groups have reported and comments are recorded.

Analyzing KSA Analysis Data

This step is also almost identical to the activity analysis. The list of KSAs should be analyzed for common themes and grouped according to these themes. Usually the list can be reduced by some selective clustering. Then the group is asked, "If managers know these KSAs at the end of a training program, would they be able to do the activities defined earlier for this competency?" If the answer is yes, the group's work is done. If the answer is no, the group adds KSAs until they can answer yes.

Determining the Best Development Strategy

Leadership competencies may be developed through formal learning experiences (such as training) or by on-the-job developmental experiences, or a combination of the two. Any on-the-job experiences should be as systematic and deliberate as any formal planned learning activity (Jacobs & Jones, 1995). The KSAs for each subcompetency or activity should be analyzed to determine which ones are best provided through training versus on-the-job developmental experiences.

Assembling the Course Development Team

A small team of content experts and course designers will be needed to create appropriate course units for each learning objective. They will usually not be the same people used in earlier steps, though a few may overlap. Their job is to use their subject matter expertise to identify the content to be taught and design an effective training program.

Step 5: Implementing System Improvements

The implementation of a new leadership development program requires careful thought and planning. Usually considerable effort must be devoted to communicating the benefits of the new program and marketing it to important stakeholders. The development planning group selected in Step One can often be used as ambassadors for the new program. However, one must be sure to share ownership and credit for the improvements with the stakeholders who helped develop it. As the implementation proceeds, it is important to monitor the progress of changes. In addition, plans should be made for periodic reassessments of the competency model. Competency models are dynamic systems that adapt to and flex with changing organizational conditions.

Structuring the Program

Another issue that must be resolved relates to the structure of the program. Most organizations will want to structure their program in a hierarchical manner so that competencies are developed as individuals advance through management levels. It would clearly be impossible and unnecessary to have entry-level managers develop all of these competencies at one time.

The development planning group may also be used to design the hierarchical structure of the program. The question to pose to the group is, "At what job level should each competency be taught?" A simple answer might be to teach individual-level competencies to first-line supervisors, add process-level competencies when leaders reach the next higher level of management, and add organization-level competencies when they reach the next management level above that one. In reality, the answer is likely to be more complex. A matrix should be developed that clearly indicates which competencies should be associated with which job level in the manager-leader career path. It would not be uncommon to find some competencies split between job levels, with basic-level competency developed at one point in an individual's career and more advanced competency developed later.

The second structural issue is a more fundamental one. High-performance organizations increasingly are asking for leadership to occur at all levels of the organization, not just in management positions (Bergmann, Hurson, & Russ-Eft, 1999). From this perspective, every individual in an organization has the potential to lead in some capacity, even if he or she does not formally supervise employees. For example, a staff person might take on a leadership role on a project team yet have no formal management role. Others go further to say that "in winning companies, leading and teaching are considered so essential to success that they aren't reserved for a favored few in the executive suite. . . . They nurture, and expect, leadership everywhere" (Tichy, 1997, p. 12). Every organization must make a conscious decision as to whether leadership competencies will be developed only in those located in formal leadership (management) positions or will be viewed as competencies to be distributed as widely as possible in the organization.

Putting Performance into the Development Process

Although we have focused on building competency to lead for organizational performance, the development process itself must be approached from a performance perspective. This means that the process should result in leadership performance, not just skill building. In one sense, this simply parallels the general emphasis in human resource development on performance-based training (Brethower & Smalley, 1998). This approach extends the traditional classroom training model to incorporate the transfer of learned skills into job performance and the development of effective performance systems to support the transfer of learning (Holton, 1999; Holton, Bates, & Ruona, in press).

Leadership and management development professionals increasingly are focusing on breaking down the barriers between classroom training and job performance. These efforts have explored combining work and learning in a single process. Examples include experiential and natural experiential learning (Mailick & Stumpf, 1998), action learning (Dotlich & Noel, 1998; Marquardt & Revans, 1998), work-based learning (Raelin, 2000), and strategic leadership initiatives (Conger & Benjamin, 1999). These approaches all operate from the premise that through proper facilitation, learning and direct application to organizational problems can be combined to achieve immediate bottom-line results. Transfer of learning becomes a less urgent problem because work application is built into the learning.

Regardless of which strategy is used, performance-based leadership development directly plans for job application of competencies acquired through training and development. Performance outcomes from leadership development are unlikely to occur if the development strategy itself is not grounded in performance.

The Promise of Performance-Based Leadership Development

Leadership development is at best an uncertain arena of practice. As Fred Fiedler, one of leadership's preeminent scholars, put it, "While the number of training programs is considerable and continues to grow at an increasing pace, the scarcity of sound research on training has been one of the most glaring shortcomings in the leadership area. Most of the training programs are untested, and, at best, of uncertain value" (Fiedler, 1996, p. 243). Burke and Day (1986) reinforced this point in their meta-analysis of seventy managerial and supervisory training programs, which found that only eleven used any type of objective performance outcome measure.

It is rather astonishing to realize that leadership theory has never directly incorporated performance theory or performance outcomes as core constructs. The competency model developed here represents a fundamentally different approach to developing a behavioral model of leadership. This project began with a theory of performance, not leadership. Our research question was to ask what leadership behaviors are needed to achieve desired performance outcomes and to lead each element of an organizational performance system. Thus, we asked not what leaders *do now* but what leaders *should do* to achieve effective performance.

This competency model was built from theory and research and is informed by practice. As such, we cannot be sure that outstanding performance will occur when it is implemented. However, we are sure that a commitment to performance-based leadership competency development is more likely to lead to performance effectiveness than other approaches. Much is known about performance and performance systems in organizations, and much is known about leadership in organizations. It seems only logical that connecting the two streams of research has the potential to create more effective leadership development.

References

Bergmann, H., Hurson, K., & Russ-Eft, D. (1999). *Everyone a leader: A grassroots model for the new workplace.* New York: Wiley.

Brethower, D., & Smalley, K. (1998). *Performance-based instruction: Linking training to business results.* San Francisco: Jossey-Bass.

Burke, M. J., & Day, R. R. (1986). A cumulative study of the effectiveness of managerial training. *Journal of Applied Psychology, 71*, 232–245.

Conger, J. A., & Benjamin, B. (1999). *Building leaders: How successful companies develop the next generation.* San Francisco: Jossey-Bass.

Cummings, T. G., & Worley, C. (1997). *Organizational development and change* (6th ed.) Cincinnati, OH: South-Western College Publishing.

Dotlich, D. L., & Noel, J. L. (1998). *Action learning: How the world's top companies are re-creating their leaders and themselves.* San Francisco: Jossey-Bass.

Fiedler, F. E. (1996). Research on leadership selection and training: One view of the future. *Administrative Science Quarterly, 41*, 241–250.

Holton, E. F. III (1999). Performance theory: Bounding the domains. *Performance Improvement Quarterly, 12* (3), 95–118.

Holton, E. F. III, Bates, R. A., & Ruona, W. E. A. (in press). Development of a generalized learning transfer system inventory. *Human Resource Development Quarterly.*

Jacobs, R. L., & Jones, M. J. (1995). *Structured on-the-job training: Unleashing employee expertise in the workplace.* San Francisco: Berrett-Koehler.

Mailick, S., & Stumpf, S. A. (1998). *Learning theory in the practice of management development: Evolution and application.* Westport, CT: Quorum Books.

Marquardt, M. J., & Revans, R. (1999). *Action learning in action: Transforming problems and people for world-class organizational learning.* Palo Alto, CA: Davies-Black Publishing.

Raelin, J. A. (2000). *Work-based learning: The new frontier of management development.* Upper Saddle River, NJ: Prentice Hall.

Tichy, N. M. (1997). *The leadership engine.* New York: HarperCollins.

Index
▲ ▲ ▲

Carson R. Arnett has more than twenty-five years of experience in training and development. He currently serves as the manager of the Academy of Human Resource Development and is a Ph.D. candidate in human resource development at Louisiana State University

Debora E. Baker is the director of residential life at Louisiana State University. She has worked in the field of college student housing for seventeen years. She is currently pursuing a Ph.D. in human resource development at Louisiana State University.

Mary Allyn Boudreaux has been employed by Louisiana State University for over twenty years and currently serves as a coordinator in the Academic Center for Athletes. She is pursuing a doctorate in human resource development at Louisiana State University.

Doris B. Collins is associate vice chancellor for student life and academic services at Louisiana State University. She is a nationally recognized consultant in college student affairs, has served as president of the Association of College and University Housing Officers–International, has participated in national teleconferences, and has chaired national committees and task forces on issues related to services and programs offered on college campuses. She is a Ph.D. candidate in human resource development at Louisiana State University.

Mertis Edwards is the director of quality and employee development for the City of Baton Rouge, Parish of East Baton Rouge, where she conducts performance and training needs analysis and designs and delivers training for city and parish employees. She is enrolled in Louisiana State University's Ph.D. program in human resource development

Elwood F. Holton III, Ed.D., is professor of human resource development at Louisiana State University, where he also coordinates the HRD degree programs. He is also the immediate past president of the Academy of Human Resource Development. Holton serves on a variety of editorial boards, has published over one hundred articles in leading HRD journals, and has authored or edited eight books. He has consulted with a wide variety of private, public, and nonprofit organizations on HRD and performance improvement issues.

Janis S. Lowe is assistant secretary for the Louisiana Department of Economic Development and heads the Office of Policy and Research. She is enrolled in the Ph.D. program at Louisiana State University in human resource development.

Susan A. Lynham is a Ph.D. candidate in human resource development at the University of Minnesota. Her areas of scholarly interest and research focus on methods of theory building and theory building research in HRD and on strategic HRD, specifically leadership and leadership development for performance. She has more than sixteen years of experience as an HRD professional, gained in both South Africa and the United States. A significant part of her professional experience has involved the analysis, design, development, and implementation of executive and senior-management-level leadership development processes and programs.

Lori Marjerison is a certified SAP HR consultant with IBM's GlobalServices' ERP Practice. She has over eleven years of human resource management experience in the service sector, with heavy emphasis on improving HR business processes.

Sharon S. Naquin, Ph.D., is director of the Office of Human Resource Development Research at Louisiana State University, where her primary research has focused on dispositional effects on adult learning in the workplace. She has served as the lead researcher on HRD research grants in the areas of organizational needs analysis, community workforce development systems, business and industry needs assessment, and management development evaluation. In addition, she has eleven years of experience in corporate human resources.

Marie B. Walsh is enrolled in the human resource development Ph.D. program at Louisiana State University. She has over fifteen years of project management, supervisory, and management experience in the private and public sectors. She is currently a senior training and development analyst for the Baton Rouge City-Parish government.

Lynda S. Wilson is the director of human resources for West TeleServices and is enrolled in the HRD program at Louisiana State University, where she is pursuing a Ph.D. She earned SPHR certification in human resource management in 1997 and has thirteen years of experience in the human resource field.

Academy of Human Resource Development

The Academy of Human Resource Development (AHRD) is a global organization made up of, governed by, and created for the human resource development (HRD) scholarly community of academics and reflective practitioners. The Academy was formed to encourage systematic study of human resource development theories, processes, and practices; to disseminate information about HRD; to encourage the application of HRD research findings; and to provide opportunities for social interaction among individuals with scholarly and professional interests in HRD from multiple disciplines and from across the globe.

AHRD membership includes a subscription to *Advances in Developing Human Resources, Human Resource Development Quarterly,* and *Human Resource Development International.* A partial list of other benefits includes (1) membership in the only global organization dedicated to advancing the HRD profession through research, (2) annual research conference with full proceedings of research papers (900 pages), (3) reduced prices on professional books, (4) subscription to the *Forum,* the academy newsletter, and (5) research partnering, funding, and publishing opportunities. Senior practitioners are encouraged to join AHRD's Global 100!

Academy of Human Resource Development
P.O. Box 25113
Baton Rouge, LA 70894-511
USA

Phone: 225-334-1874
Fax: 225-334-1875
E-mail: office@ahrd.org
Website: http://www.ahrd.org

Check out Berrett-Koehler's new website:
www.bkconnection.com

✔ Special Internet-only discounts
✔ Pre-publication previews of new books
✔ Exclusive articles available only on our site
✔ And more!

BERRETT-KOEHLER is pleased to announce the launch of our new website at www.bkconnection.com. One of our primary purposes at Berrett-Koehler has been to build and sustain a community of readers, customers, and other stakeholders who are committed to creating a more enlightened world of work and more open, effective, and humane organizations. We have created this website to serve as a hub for that community. This new site features:

Advance previews and special discounts
- Savings of up to 30% on new releases and special offers
- The latest e-commerce technology which ensures safe and secure online ordering
- A complete catalog—everything we've ever published, searchable by author and title
- Excerpts from new and forthcoming books: Currently we are featuring a preview of the new, revised and expanded edition of Margaret Wheatley's classic *Leadership and the New Science*. If you haven't read it, find out why the first edition sold over 200,000 copies and was named one of the top ten books of the past decade by *CIO Magazine* and one of the top ten business books of all time by Xerox Business Services. If you have read it, find out what's new in the revised and expanded edition, share your thoughts about the book with other readers, and discover how you can start a *Leadership and the New Science* discussion group.

Exclusive information available nowhere else
- "Think Tank," a section featuring articles by some of the most innovative thinkers in business today—including Alan Briskin, Hazel Henderson, Barbara Moses, Sam Stern, and many others
- A "Tip-of-the-Week" section where you'll find practical tips from renowned experts on a range of important topics—from how to telecommute effectively to how to have more fun in the office
- Reading group materials—including free downloadable discussion guides and an opportunity to obtain free books to get your group started
- A searchable directory of leading experts and speakers, serving as a direct link between you and the experts
- BK's own "Innovative Practices Awards"—links to organizations we believe are helping to lead the way to a more humane workplace

At our recent Berrett-Koehler Community Dialog, BK author Harrison Owen *(Open Space Technology, Expanding Our Now,* and *The Spirit of Leadership)* commented that "the best way to build community is to provide space for community to happen." We hope that bkconnection.com will be such a space. We value your feedback, so please visit us today at www.bkconnection.com and let us know what you think.

Using *Advances in Developing Human Resources* as a Text

The size and style of each issue of *Advances* makes it perfect for use as a text for short courses and workshops, and as a supplemental text for graduate and undergraduate courses. I encourage you to consider using *Advances* in your teaching. For example, we are using issues 1 and 2 as supplemental texts at the University of Minnesota. These two monographs introduce our students to important ideas from fourteen HRD scholars.

We are using *Advances* issue #2—"Action Learning: Successful Strategies for Individual, Team, and Organizational Development" edited by Yorks, O'Neil, and Marsick—as a supplementary text in our Personnel Training and Development course. The primary texts are *Analysis for Improving Performance: Tools for Diagnosing and Documenting Workplace Expertise* by Swanson and *Structured On-the-Job Training: Unleashing Employee Expertise in the Workplace* by Jacobs and Jones.

For our Strategic Planning in HRD course, we are using *Advances* issue #1—"Performance Improvement Theory and Practice" edited by Torraco—as a supplementary text. The primary text is *Improving Performance: Managing the White Space in Organizations* by Rummler and Brache, along with other readings on strategy, scenario building, systems thinking, and quality.

Anyone interested in the syllabi for these two courses should send me an e-mail at raswanson@uswest.net. I would also like to hear from you how you are using the *Advances* monographs.

Richard A. Swanson
Editor-in-Chief

Advances in Developing Human Resources

ADVANCES in Developing Human Resources (Advances) is a new and unique kind of HRD publication—a quarterly series of paperbacks, each one focused on a single important topic such as performance improvement, action learning, on-the-job training, intellectual capital, globalization, downsizing, and diversity.

These monographs are edited by, and feature contributions from, some of the top minds in HRD today. Each contributor brings his or her particular expertise to bear on one aspect of the volume's topic.

So each volume in the series is like a seminar in print. You don't just get one person's perspective on one aspect of a topic—you get a complete picture of state-of-the-art thought and practice in a critical area of HRD.

ADVANCES will be an invaluable tool in helping you to develop HRD policies and practices that are rooted in the most forward-looking HRD thinking.

Performance Improvement Theory and Practice
(Advances 1)
Richard Torraco, Editor

1. Theoretical Foundations of Performance Improvement and Implications for Practice, *Richard A. Swanson* 2. Performance Domains and Their Boundaries, *Elwood F. Holton III* 3. Measuring Performance Improvement, *Reid A. Bates* 4. Research Methods for Advancing Performance Improvement, *Darlene Russ-Eft* 5. Case Studies in Performance Improvement, *Martin Mulder* 6. Advancing our Understanding of Performance Improvement, *Richard J. Torraco* 124 pages (March 1999) ISBN 1-58376-011-3

Action Learning: Successful Strategies for Individual, Team, and Organizational Development
(Advances 2)
Lyle Yorks, Judy O'Neil, & Victoria J. Marsick, Editors

1. Action Learning: Theoretical Bases and Varieties of Practice, *Lyle Yorks, Judy O'Neil, Victoria Marsick* 2. Issues in the Design and Implementation of an Action Learning Initiative, *Judy O'Neil, Robert L. Dilworth* 3. Facilitating Action Learning: The Role of the Learning Coach, *Judy O'Neil* 4. Action Learning for Personal and Transformational Learning, *Robert L. Dilworth, Verna J. Willis* 5. Transfer of Learning from Action Learning Programs to the Organizational Setting, *Lyle Yorks, Sharon Lamm, Judy O'Neil* 6. Organizational Culture Change Through Action Learning, *Glenn Nilson* 7. Action Learning Lessons for

Management Development and Organizational Learning, *Lyle Yorks, Judy O'Neil, Victoria Marsick* 8. Annotated Bibliography, *Mary Ragno* 124 pages (June 1999) ISBN: 1-58376-022-9

Informal Learning on the Job
(Advances 3)
Victoria J. Marsick & Marie Volpe, Editors

1. The Nature of and Need for Informal Learning, *Marie Volpe, Victoria J. Marsick* 2. Learning Informally in the Aftermath of Downsizing, *Marie Volpe* 3. Learning Partnerships, *Barbara Keelor (Larson) Lovin* 4. Learning to Be an Effective Team Member, *Sally Vernon* 5. How Managers Learn in the Knowledge Era, *Kathleen Dechant* 6. "Awakening": Developing Learning Capacity in a Small Family Business, *Mary Ziegler* 7. Critical Reflection as a Response to Organizational Disruption, *Ann K. Brooks* 8. Theory and Practice of Informal Learning in the Knowledge Era, *Victoria J. Marsick, Marie Volpe, Karen E. Watkins* 124 pages (September 1999) ISBN 1-58376-023-7

Developing Human Resources in the Global Economy
(Advances 4)
Michael J. Marquardt, Editor

1. Revitalizing HRD for the New Global Millennium, *Mary McAleese* 2. Preparing Human Resources for the Global Economy, *Michael J. Marquardt, Francesco Sofo* 3. Developing Leaders for a Global Consumer Products Company, *Jill Conner, Michael J. Marquardt* 4. Human Resource Issues in Russia: A Case Study, *Nancy O. Berger* 5. The Impact of Globalization on Managerial Learning: The Case of Romania, *Maria Cseh* 6. Individual and Organizational Learning of Chinese Executives at Compaq-China, *Wong Wee Chwee* 7. The Challenges of Globalization and the HRD Response, *Annette Hartenstein* 124 pages (December 1999) ISBN 1-58376-024-5

Strategic Perspectives on Knowledge, Competence, and Expertise
(Advances 5)
Richard W. Herling & Joanne Provo, Editors

1. Knowledge, Competence, and Expertise in Organizations, *Richard W. Herling, Joanne Provo* 2. Operational Definitions of Expertise and Competence, *Richard W. Herling* 3. A Theory of Intellectual Capital, *Louise Harris* 4. A Theory of Knowledge Management, *Richard J. Torraco* 5. Training as a Strategic Investment, *Richard A. Krohn* 6. Measuring Human Capital, *Joanne Provo* 7. Knowledge Management and Strategic Planning, *Oscar A. Aliaga* 124 pages (March 2000) ISBN 1-58376-057-1

A dvances in Developing Human Resources

ORDER FORM

For fastest service, order online through our secure server at bkconnection.com
Call toll-free 7 AM to 12 Midnight: 800-929-2929   Fax to 802-864-7626
Or mail to Berrett-Koeher Communications, PO Box 565, Williston, VT 05495

Subscription to Advances in Developing Human Resources (Item no. 34223-611)

[ ] Individual- $79   [ ] Institutional- $125

For subscription orders outside the United States, please add $15 for surface mail or $30 for air mail.

Single issues: $19.95 each

_____ #1, Performance Improvement: Theory and Practice (item no. 60113-611)
_____ #2, Action Learning: Successful Strategies for Individual, Team, and
          Organizational Development (item no. 60229-611)
_____ #3, Informal Learning on the Job (item no. 60237-611)
_____ #4, Developing Human Resources in the Global Economy (item no. 60245-611)

Quantity discounts on purchases of 10 or more copies of a single title are available. Call Berrett-Koehler Special Sales for more information at 415-288-0260

$ _____ Subtotal
$ _____ Shipping and Handling ($4.50 for one issue, $1.50 for each additional issue)
$ _____ In CA add sales tax
$ _____ Total (Note: No shipping and handling or sales tax on subscriptions.)

Method of Payment

[ ] Payment Enclosed
[ ] Bill me (purchase order number required)   P.O. number _____
[ ] VISA   [ ] MasterCard   [ ] American Express

Card No. _____   Exp. Date _____

Signature _____

Name _____   Title _____

Address _____

City, State, Zip _____

Bill to (if different from Ship to): _____

Name _____   Title _____

Address _____

City, State, Zip _____

Be the first to hear about new publications, special discount offers, exclusive articles, and more! Join the Berrett-Koehler e-mail list!

Your e-mail address _____

Campaign code = 611

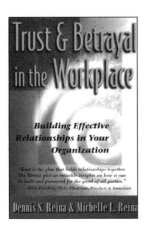

Building Effective Relationships in Your Organization

"Trust is the glue that holds relationships together. The Reinas give us valuable insights on how it can be built and preserved for the good of all parties."
—Price Pritchett, Ph.D., Chairman, Pritchett & Associates

Dennis S. Reina & Michelle L. Reina

Hardcover, 188 pages
November 1999
ISBN 1-57675-070-1
Item no. 50701-602
$27.95

Trust and Betrayal in the Workplace
Building Effective Relationships in
Your Organization
Dennis S. Reina and Michelle L. Reina

- Presents a powerful new research-based model for building trust and healing individuals, teams, and organizations from betrayal
- The first book to identify and define the three kinds of Transactional Trust in a practical framework that can be easily applied to workplace relationships
- Provides Ideas in Action exercises, tips, and real-life examples that illustrate trust-building principles and practices at work

Trust in the workplace is more important than ever. If organizations are going to survive in the new global economy, their employees must trust themselves and their leaders enough to be willing to take the risks necessary to adapt to the rapidly changing conditions of the marketplace. But after two decades of downsizing, restructuring, and managerial changes, trust within American organizations has reached an all-time low. How can leaders reverse the damage?

Trust and Betrayal in the Workplace provides proven steps to help leaders, employees, and their organizations acknowledge betrayal, solidly recover from it, and rebuild trust. Through in-depth, practical guidelines it clearly explains the dynamics of trust and helps organization members develop a common language to discuss trust-related issues, to identify behaviors that build trust and behaviors that break trust, and to take action on trust-related issues. It provides suggestions, behaviors, and exercises that can be put to use immediately to begin building effective work relationships, productive work environments, and healthy bottom lines.

Trust and Betrayal in the Workplace tells readers everything they need to know about trust: the power unleashed when it exists, the problems created when it doesn't, and the pain suffered when it is betrayed. Through a powerful model that has been successfully applied in organizations in a wide variety of industries, it shows leaders at all levels how to begin the process of healing from betrayal and build an environment that supports trust within themselves, their employees, and their organizations.

To order call toll-free: **(800) 929-2929**
Internet: www.bkpub.com   Fax: 802-864-7627   Or mail to
Berrett-Koehler Publishers, P.O. Box 565, Williston VT 05495

Berrett-Koehler
San Francisco

Paperback original, 394 pages
July 1999
ISBN 1-57675-058-2
Item no. 50852-602
$49.95

The Change Handbook
Group Methods for Shaping the Future
Peggy Holman and Tom Devane, Editors

The Change Handbook presents 18 proven change methods together in a single volume. Each method is described in a separate chapter, written by its creator or an expert practitioner. The authors lay out the distinctive aspects of each method, including a story that illustrates its use; answers to frequently asked questions; tips for getting started; an outline of roles, responsibilities, and relationships; impact on power and authority; conditions for success; theory or research base; and keys to sustaining results. The book also includes a comparative matrix that readers can use as a quick reference for understanding the distinctions among methods.

BERRETT
BK Berrett-Koehler
KOEHLER San Francisco

To order call toll-free: **(800) 929-2929**

Internet: www.bkpub.com   Fax: 802-864-7627   Or mail to

Berrett-Koehler Publishers, P.O. Box 565, Williston VT 05495

Collaborating for Change

Adapted from chapters in *The Change Handbook*, *The Collaborating for Change* booklet series offers concise, comprehensive overviews of 14 leading change strategies in a convenient, inexpensive format. Each booklet is approximately 48 pages long and includes thought-provoking questions for discussion.

Search Conference
Merrelyn Emrey and Tom Devane
ISBN 58376-034-2   Item no. 60342-602 $8.95

Future Search
Marvin R. Weisbord and Sandra Janoff
ISBN 58376-035-0   Item no. 60350-602 $8.95

Strategic Forum
Chris Soderquist
ISBN 58376-036-9   Item no. 60369-602 $8.95

Participative Design Workshop
Merrelyn Emery and Tom Devane
ISBN 58376-037-7   Item no. 60377-602 $8.95

Gemba Kaizen
Masaaki Imai and Brian Haymans
ISBN 58376-038-5   Item no. 60385-602 $8.95

Whole Systems Approach
Cindy Adams and W. A. (Bill) Adams
ISBN 58376-039-3   Item no. 60393-602 $8.95

Preferred Futuring
Lawrence L. Lippitt
ISBN 58376-040-7   Item no. 60407-602 $8.95

Organization Workshop
Barry Oshry
ISBN 58376-041-5   Item no. 60415-602 $8.95

Whole-Scale Change
Kathleen D. Dannemiller, Sylvia L. James, and Paul D. Tolchinsky
ISBN 58376-042-3   Item no. 60423-602 $8.95

Open Space Technology
Harrison Owen (with Anne Stadler)
ISBN 58376-043-1   Item no. 60431-602 $8.95

Appreciative Inquiry
David L. Cooperrider and Diana Whitney
ISBN 58376-044-X   Item no. 6044X-602 $8.95

Conference Model
Emily and Dick Axelrod
ISBN 58376-045-8   Item no. 60458-602 $8.95

Think Like a Genius
Todd Siler
ISBN 58376-046-6   Item no. 60466-602 $8.95

Real Time Strategic Change
Robert W. Jacobs and Frank McKeown
ISBN 58376-047-4   Item no. 60474-602 $8.95

Berrett-Koehler
San Francisco

To order call toll-free: **(800) 929-2929**

Internet: www.bkpub.com   Fax: 802-864-7627   Or mail to

Berrett-Koehler Publishers, P.O. Box 565, Williston VT 05495

St. Thomas Aquinas College
Lougheed Library
125 Route 304, Sparkill, NY 10976-1050

The St. Thomas Aquinas College
National Center
For Ethics and Social Responsibility

Date Due
